TED
SHAWN

FATHER
OF
AMERICAN
DANCE

TED SHAWN

FATHER OF AMERICAN DANCE

A Biography By

WALTER TERRY

The Dial Press · New York 1976

Manufactured in the United States of America

First printing

Library of Congress Cataloging in Publication Data

Terry, Walter.
   Ted Shawn, father of American dance.

   Includes index.
   1. Shawn, Ted, 1891–1972. 2. Dancing.
GV1785.S5T47   793.3'2'0924 [B]   76-13200
ISBN 0-8037-8557-7

For
Stuart
Sebastian

With gratitude to the university student whose assignment it was to assist me with sorting and cataloguing massive amounts of research materials for the preparation of this book, and with my personal thanks to this twenty-four-year-old dancer-choreographer for aiding me in deciding just how to present the significance of Ted Shawn to a new generation of theater-artists and theatergoers. These duties he performed very definitely *summa cum laude*.

Acknowledgments

I am grateful not only to Stuart Sebastian for saving me hours of time by scouring through thousands of pages of manuscripts, reviews, releases, and letters to dig up what I set for him to find but also to Dr. Girard Franklin for giving me hours of his time in which to discuss Shawn, the man; to Tony Charmoli and William Milié for reminising with me about their Shawn days; to Mme. La Meri and Myra Kinch for their very special recollections and to the many other dancers who, off and on over the years, have said a word or two to me about Ted Shawn; and, of course, to Foster Fitz-Simons, my college roommate, who said, "Let's see what this dance stuff is all about"; and to Phoebe Barr, who taught me what it was all about and introduced me to Ted Shawn.

TED
SHAWN

FATHER
OF
AMERICAN
DANCE

Prospectus for a New Prometheus

In writing my book about Ted Shawn, I sought for and found a guiding image: Prometheus *Un*bound. It fits, it seems to me, a very complex man with a simple mission. It was arrived at after months of self-search and research. It came, of course, in a flash as the assortment of images, of ideas, of dance titles, of definitions fell into place. Many of Ted Shawn's most ardent followers thought of him as a god. In fact a reviewer had once described his walk across the stage as that of a god. His detractors thought of him as a trickster. He was both in a Promethean sense.

Prometheus was the Titan who stole fire from the gods to give to mankind. He was the bringer, not the giver, of light. His very name is pertinent for it means literally "Forethinker." Ted Shawn was that certainly. No one ever questioned his intellectual side. But Prometheus had another side. His Norse equivalent, to whom he has been compared by classical scholars, is Loki, a member of the highest hierarchy of gods but ofttimes an embarrassing trickster. Ted Shawn was both.

Shawn, like Isadora Duncan, was drawn to the Greek ideal of body beauty and to the heroic nature of classical Greek drama, myths, and history itself. Of all of his many dances for himself two of his favorites were *The Divine Idiot*, based on Plato's shadow watchers. Shawn introduced into the group the rebel, the prophet, the messiah perhaps, one who has seen the light of the world and would bring it to the unbelievers chained in darkness in a cave of ignorance; and *Prometheus Bound*. The former was created in 1930; the latter, the year before. They came at a crucial time in his life. The break with his wife, Ruth St. Denis, who had never let him forget that she was the superstar, was imminent. He was nearing forty and experiencing a new assurance that he had indeed become a leader. But what sort of a leader?

He occasionally in a program note described his *Prometheus Bound* as "a study in limitation." He meant it as a guide to the self-imposed choreographic challenge which required that he perform the entire solo while chained by his left arm to a massive rock on a mountainside. The description was prophetic, as was the dance itself, because it came to symbolize the paradoxical features of a man with severe limitations yet possessed of "forethought," inexhaustible energy, invincible drive. Without the innate artistic talent of either a Ruth St. Denis or an Isadora Duncan he became a coequal force in the birth and evolution of the contemporary dance in America—in some respects, truth to tell, his influences proved more permanent and more usable than those of his rivals-colleagues, the "two great dance matriarchs" as Martha Graham has called them.

In writing a biography an author quite naturally would report on the conflicting nature of his subject. Since I knew Ted Shawn well for forty years, it would not be presumptuous to speculate on why he succeeded against certain inherent odds and why he failed to achieve the recognition of great artistry which he felt he deserved. I would like to report on him, speculate about him, even interpret him to a degree. But I could not possibly "footnote" him. I leave that to pedants and scholars. Of course I want to relate him to his era— Ruth St. Denis once said to me, "You know Teddy and I were the era of roses and veils and even round-cheeked kewpie dolls, and America loved us"—and to the trends in music and painting and literature. One could delve into a relationship between New York City's famed Flatiron Building and a dance innovator or the then fashionable Vantine's (makers of incense) and Ruth St. Denis's historic solo *The Incense* or Martha Graham and Sigmund Freud, but for me, the man himself, tempestuous, temperamental, arrogant, desperately in need of love, ruthless, practical, and visionary is what Ted Shawn is all about.

The indexing, appendixing, footnoting scholar does not believe in magic. I do. For there is magic in the paramountcy of personality. How else explain those performances in Martha Graham's *Letter to the World* in those "Dear March, Come In!" scenes when Merce Cunningham was soaring heavenward and one could not take his eyes

off Graham who simply sat on a bench and cast her eyes heavenward?
I once asked the great Russian-American prima ballerina Alexandra
Danilova what the difference would be between a very fine dancer—
a soloist—and a real ballerina—it was to be a definition of the word
"ballerina." She thought a moment, her eyes lit up and in her heavy
accent she said, "Ah! Ballet is *Giselle*. Door of cottage open. Pretty
young soloist come out. You happy and you say 'I hope she do well.'
Another performance. Is also *Giselle*. Door open. Alicia Markova step
out. She not danced yet. One step only, but you sigh and say, 'Ah!
ballerina!' You do not ask, you know. She is star. She shine." Personality, of course. Magic, in truth.

The scholar too likes to put the artist into a context. The artist did
this because of this influence, that concept, those social or esthetic
situations. Frankly I believe that most of the truly great artists of
various lands and centuries didn't know what the hell they were
doing. A superficial relating of them to concurrent activities is un-
fair. What happened was profound, what they created came from
deep within, something like Minerva from the head of Jove. Isadora
didn't know what she was doing nor did St. Denis. They just did
what they *had* to do.

Ted Shawn's most famous, and distinguished, creation for his
company of Men Dancers was his *Kinetic Molpai*, a philosophical work
in which he explored, according to his own program notes, "Love,
Strife, Death, and that which is beyond Death." But this, the most
admired of this group works, did not start out that way. His composer-pianist, Jess Meeker, told me that Shawn had been working on
a series of technique training studies designed to help the dancers develop facility in matters of resilience, spinal successions, falls, opposing movements, parallel movements, jumps, and so on. A friend of
Shawn's, a philosopher and Greek scholar, saw these etudes and said
something to this effect: "My God, Ted, here is the *molpê* reborn!"
Ted rushed to the classical dictionary to find out what *molpê* meant.
It was the final celebration which took place on the threshing floors
of ancient Greece when the harvest was done, when the men had
threshed the grain with their feet and when they danced their thanks
for nature's largesse. Ted found the plural was *molpai*. His *molpai* did
not use words of prayer and praise but said it all in movement. That
would be kinetics. Thus, *Kinetic Molpai* was born. Ted Shawn had

not known what he was doing. But he had done it. It worked. It was a masterpiece. As a matter of fact it was truly *molpê* (and very definitely kinetic).

Like Duncan, St. Denis, and the other true geniuses, Ted Shawn had personality, he had instinct (he didn't know always what he was creating but he knew where he was going), he had dedication, and he was messianic. But unlike the others, he was organized. He was prepared to channel his dance discoveries into a usable mold, to organize his materials and his talents, his theories and his credos into what might be described as the curriculum of a career. A small example: St. Denis, in the brilliant "Delirium of the Senses" episode in *Radha*, whirls in ecstasy. No one had ever taught her how to turn; she spun in wild self-enchantment because the theme called for it. Ted Shawn also knew that some turns, unlike the feats of prowess exhibited by the spinning ballet dancer, were manifestations of spiritual ecstasy. He even, in such solos as his *Mevlevi Dervish*, communicated that self-induced ecstasy, but he knew *how* to turn.

In Denishawn classes my own dance teacher (a Denishawn product) would say, "Miss Ruth would come in with all her drapes and say to us students, 'Dears, we'll *feel* turns today. The spiral form of rhythm is man's most spiritual expression.' And somehow we'd find ourselves kind of hypnotized and able to turn as beautifully as she did. Then she'd sweep out and we'd find we hadn't learned a thing. But then Papa Shawn would come in and say, 'What did Miss Ruth teach you today?' We'd tell him and he'd say, 'Okay, now here is the principle of the turn. Put your right foot flat on the floor, the left is waiting for a lift on half-toe, hold your body, etc.' And when he was through, we knew how to turn." St. Denis brought the magic; Shawn, the method.

Shawn always resented the cliché that his wife was the spirit and he the form of their joint Denishawn adventure in choreographies, companies, schools, curricula. He was right in resenting the description, for he was much more than that. He was the catalyst who fused inspiration and accomplishment.

But why should I choose the image for this biography of Ted Shawn as Prometheus *Un*bound and not the exact title of his dance which clearly states and, in the staging, shows *bound?* Well, there is, of course, an anecdote—there were always anecdotes with the Denishawners. Ted was performing *Prometheus Bound* on one occasion when there was an accident of truly Titanic proportions. The prop—the huge rock to which the figure was chained—was pretty old by the time this particular revival rolled around. The dancer was chained not only by his left arm but also by his right leg. Thus he could, though restricted in a certain sense, move into precarious, off-balance positions without fear of falling. This time, however, the screws for the chains on the leg eased out of the rotting wood as the dancer pulled and struggled against his fetters. According to Shawn—I missed that show—he hurtled into space, held to the rock only by one chained arm, spun around the mountainside, recovered his footing, and never missed a beat.

He adored telling this story of near disaster and how he had triumphed, just as he relished the report of how he went on stage every night on tour in his *The Cosmic Dance of Shiva*, requiring all manner of spinal flexibilities and related actions, while his sacroiliac was painfully out of place.

These true tales, slightly dramatized, were typical of him. So when I recalled this story of the brink-defying performance of *Prometheus*, I thought how like him to do the gods one better. But it wasn't just bravado on his part. Prometheus. Bound or Unbound? Yes, Ted Shawn reproduced within himself the spirit of the ancient Prometheus with its messianic desire to bring light to others. But Ted Shawn, dancer, was fettered by his own physical limitations—he was not blessed with the dancer's ideal build of slim litheness—and his own esthetic and artistic lacks. But he would not be bound. He literally, as in the unexpected performance, tore himself free, at least partly, of his bonds and swung out into a career for which the gods had not endowed him. To make a lasting impact on the entire world of dance he had to become a new kind of Prometheus, a Prometheus *unbound*. And that is what he became.

1

He looked across the room and in the dimness he saw a shape, a form. It fascinated him because he wasn't quite sure what it was or, more to the point, who it was. Over the years he had, in fantasy, glanced into this mysterious corner of his life where this constantly changing shape intrigued him, hypnotized him, and at times angered him by its very elusiveness. "One day," he said, "I had the courage to turn on a bright light and look. It was nothing more than the equivalent of an old coat tossed onto a chair. As a matter of fact, it was my wife, Ruth St. Denis. And in that instant of revelation, all her magic, her mystery, her power over me disappeared forever. She was just an old coat."

Said St. Denis of her husband Ted Shawn, "But he never loved the old coat. He didn't marry a rather sloppy farm girl from New Jersey. He married a goddess. She didn't exist, except on the stage. The deception was of his own making, not mine."

The deceptions, the attractions, the jealousies, the inexplicable magnetisms and the contempts, each for the other, lasted through sixteen years of actual bed and board and spilled over into more than fifty years of marriage. Ruth St. Denis and Ted Shawn made history in the theaters and schools and classrooms of the world. They were both selfish, arrogant, grasping, untruthful, and tormented beings. They were deeply concerned with destiny but they were smart enough to know that destiny, unlike the promises of poesy, did not await them, that destiny had to be assaulted before anyone else could get to her first. Ruth St. Denis and Ted Shawn deserved each other.

In the first years of their marriage—they met, married and became theatrical partners in 1914—their sex life was highly satisfactory. Or so they said. Each one told me this on more than one occasion. It

9

was one of the few things they agreed on. St. Denis admitted—it is recorded in her journals—to extramarital flings. Shawn told me that he was absolutely faithful—except for "some fumblings"—until their separation. But were they protesting too much? Is this what they wanted the public to think? I believe not.

Ruth St. Denis would never have married Ted Shawn if she had not wanted sex with him. She knew that the American public responded with violent disapproval, and even contempt, to Isadora Duncan's love affairs and illegitimate children. "It was horrid and cheap," Ruth St. Denis wrote in her autobiography, "and cast a degrading spell on all of dance." But she confessed, "If I had been quite true to my deepest convictions at that time and not to the standard of morality which I had been mesmerized into substituting for my truer instinct, I would have lived with Ted until our physical desire for each other had been spent. . . ."

And so they were married. The physical attraction appeared to be genuine, and probably the sex desires were never fully spent, although they certainly receded. Why? Dr. Girard Franklin, psychiatrist-psychologist and one-time student at a Shawn school, believes that Ted Shawn was in search of a mother when he married the much older St. Denis. As for St. Denis herself, she soon discovered that "in our attraction for each other, where there appeared to be two, there were in reality four beings to be adjusted and unfolded. Four distinct people were found in the circle of our marriage. The masculine in me and the feminine in Ted were as much alive and as needing to be expressed as the physical man and woman which the world saw."

As the desire was spent, the wife turned to other fleeting loves, as much poetically romantic as physical (and some were simply moonlit idylls); the husband, save for the "fumblings," swore he remained faithful. But this self-imposed virtue came to an abrupt end when, after fifteen years of marriage, they moved to separate beds. This is when he discovered the old coat. This is when they both fell in love with the same man.

Ted Shawn won the wooing contest and St. Denis threatened to sue for divorce, naming the man as corespondent. This, forty years ago, would have destroyed the Shawn career. In the American provincial mind men dancers were suspect anyhow. If St. Denis had carried out her threat, which she did not, every American father would have cause to worry about a son even faintly interested in dance. Shawn's own fraternity brothers at the University of Denver in 1910 had said in shocked tones, when they learned that their classmate had left college in order to become a dancer, "But Ted, *men* don't dance."

Ted Shawn, all six feet of him, was every inch a man. In speech, manner, and etiquette he was wholly virile, a man and a gentleman. On stage, sometimes, his taste in costume or makeup would be questionable. But one must remember that he was the first American man dancer, in the art area rather than in hoofing, to come along since George Washington Smith, a classical ballet dancer, had retired in the mid-nineteenth century. As a nonballet dancer, as an "expressional" dancer, as one who wanted to restore to male dancing the dignity it had once possessed in ancient Greece, he had no one to guide him. He had been born into a world of female dance, into an era when even large-bosomed-and-bottomed women played male roles *en travesti* in ballet. Even the innovators whom he admired were women—Isadora Duncan, Loie Fuller, Ruth St. Denis. Ted Shawn, who was to fall in love with a man, fought to make dancing for men an honorable profession in America. He won the fight.

Did he seem masculine? Was there anything odd about him? I was about nineteen when I first met him, just beginning to study dance in college. He was the first star I had ever met. I was disappointed. He was big, strong, almost fatherly. Virile too, but he did not *look* like a dancer, he didn't *look* like a star. He was on a tour of one-night stands with his company, and he had stopped off briefly to see our dance teacher, a young matron who had been a member of his troupe before she retired in order to be with her professor-husband. Mr. Shawn watched us in a dance class—there were ten to fifteen boys and six or seven girls (a remarkable ratio for the 1930s!)—and we watched him. His hair was thinning and graying, his big frame (seen offstage) did not even hint at the dancer, and to us he seemed old. He was in his early forties.

A few years later I introduced him to my mother and father. (By that time I had determined upon a career in dance—as a critic.) My father had not been enthusiastic about my passion for dance but he never interfered—the minister of our church in Connecticut and his wife had convinced Dad that I knew what I was doing. I suspect now that they were wise enough to realize that someone fired with zeal—and the church knows all about that—was not to be deterred. My very practical father had long since conceded that he had lost his only son to the arts. He had hoped for literature, drama, or music. He was unhappy about dance but not for any moral reasons. He was sure that I wanted to be a dancer, and he was worried that a performing career would come to an end by thirty-five.

It is possible that he had some secret worries about the fact that Mr. Shawn had shown a great interest in me. What he didn't know was that Shawn guessed that I would never be a dancer—although he invited me to join his all-male company—because I was determined to be a writer, a writer on dance. Ted Shawn was equally determined that he would mold my mind—not touch my body—so that he would have a spokesman for his activities, opinions, and prejudices in dance. He pursued this course—with more subtlety in later years—until he died at eighty. He influenced me tremendously, but he never succeeded in making me a tool.

Mother and Dad did not know about his esthetic plans for me. When they met him, they liked him instantly and Dad was pleasurably surprised: "He looks like a highly successful businessman," he said later. "A banker." With this high praise for one of the great dance figures of all time, Dad never worried about Ted Shawn and me again.

Many years later, when we discussed the biography that I would write one day, I asked him why he went from his love affair with St. Denis to having an affair with a man. That was when he told me about the "old coat." He went on to say that his wife's infidelity had been especially insulting. "She never took a lover who was anyone at all. They were pimply-faced youths! So I decided that no woman would ever again hurt me."

This explanation seemed reasonable at the time. I knew that St. Denis had left him, returned to him, and vacillated during sixteen years of marriage. It was no secret that she was bitter about his demand for equal billing with her. Once he showed her a new solo and, sweating profusely, sat at her feet in the studio. He was asking for approval or help. She patted him on the head in front of their

Denishawn dancers and said, "Possibilities, Teddy," and swept out. On another occasion a magazine conducted a contest to see who their readers thought were the best dancers of the day. Pavlova won it for women; Shawn for men. St. Denis commented, "Well, if I had won a popularity contest, I would be quite certain I was no artist."

But the problem was deeper. At eighty Shawn looked back. He "guessed" that there had always been a tendency to homosexuality, although he was engaged to be married several times when he was young and even planned to marry again if St. Denis divorced him. But he recalled that he was attracted to handsome men, to the male body, to the Greek ideal. He believed in male-male love but he also believed equally strongly in family. The two, in his mind, were not antithetical. The Greeks of antiquity had accepted this.

But his own wife refused to have children. In fact their marriage was not consummated immediately. "Ruth," he said, "was terrified of having children. She used every birth control method invented from medieval times to the present to avoid conception. So we never had children." Perhaps that is why he was proud of being called "Papa Denishawn" and, later, simply "Papa Shawn."

In his last years he would ponder upon a career in dance that spanned half a century, take stock of it, jealously guard his own innovative contributions to dance, and overprotest his very great contributions to dance in America—indeed, Pauline Lawrence, a former Denishawner, once said with more than a touch of irony, "Oh come on now, Ted, we all know that you invented dancing." He was irritated by the remark but he quoted it often enough to make one think he partly believed it.

As an old man he also pondered the homosexual theme. He became, of course, a philosopher and a scholar, as his books, articles, lectures, and voluminous correspondence attest. I remember his telling me that when he was a youth, he had never heard the word "homosexual"; that later it became an accepted condemnation; and that still later, society settled for it as a disease. He lived to see laws changed to protect consenting adults. He did not by any means dwell on homosexual issues—dance as an art form and as a tool in education was always first—but he felt that the condemning of a homosexual was immoral and that the punishment of a homosexual should be illegal.

I've introduced this matter into the biography of Ted Shawn not simply to stir up old questions, half-forgotten doubts, but for two reasons: (1) the moral issue was important to him and he even said to me in his last years, "Someday I will be able to speak out about this without harm to the dance or, if it is too late, maybe you'll speak for me"; (2) his actual career, as well as his personal life, was affected at various times by this homosexual element in terms of choreographies and composition of companies. If the twentieth century—his half of it—had permitted him the classical Greek acceptance (Shawn was delighted with the literary popularization of the theme in Mary Renault's *The Last of the Wine*) of husband-with-wife-and-male-lover, he would never have been uneasy about his personal life-style nor would he have suffered in behalf of frightened homosexuals that he felt were wrongly treated by society.

So the homosexual area was important to him. But it was not paramount. First and foremost Ted Shawn was an artist of the dance.

2

Edwin Myers Shawn was born October 21, 1891, in Kansas City, Missouri. His father was a successful newspaperman. His mother was related to the famous Booth family of actors. Ted was born to be an evangelist. At five he announced that he wanted to be a preacher on Sundays and Wednesdays and an actor for the rest of the week. In his career as a dancer he was often theatrically flamboyant, but he was always the dedicated evangelist for the dance cause. He exchanged a pulpit for the stage.

In fact he planned to be a Methodist minister. He had grown up in Denver, Colorado, and when he enrolled at the University of Denver, his goal was the ministry. A dance career never occurred to him. An American male earning his living as a dancer? Unthinkable! And he never thought about it. But destiny had something to say. The young university student contracted diphtheria and the experimental serum which saved his life also paralyzed him from the waist down. As he began to recover, he turned to therapy, to exercise, to restore mobility to his limbs. This led him to dance. His first teacher, in Denver, was Hazel Wallack, a ballet dancer from the Metropolitan Opera.

Ted, at college age, was a little too old to begin ballet instruction, at least as far as a dance career was concerned. He recognized this, was grateful for his ballet training, earned some money with Miss Wallack, doing exhibitions of ballroom dance styles of the day, and was told by the university's chancellor, who had once encouraged his interest in theology, that he was sorry that he, Ted, had left the university because he would have liked the opportunity to expel him. Such was the status of dance in Denver, 1911.

It is perfectly fair to pose a conjecture at this point in the story of

Ted Shawn and in the history of dance. Did he become an innovator because physical limitations made a career as a ballet dancer dubious? Or did he turn to dance innovation because he was a dance reformer? Not only did he begin ballet lessons late—in the royal and state ballet schools of Europe, students start intensive training at nine—but he was also a big man, not only in height but in weight. He often said to me in later years about his ballet possibilities that "I was much too big a man to twitter my feet."

Since Ted Shawn was always practical as well as visionary, it may be supposed that when he determined on a dance career, he analyzed ballet's demands and his own body potential and found that they were not yet altogether compatible. On the other hand, given his determination and indomitable will, he probably could have forced his body into the ballet mold. His age and his body structure certainly influenced his direction to a degree, but the major force was that innate evangelism which made him want to proclaim, and sell, dance as a major art with himself as the leader. With the trivial dance styles of his vaudeville exposures and the ballet's concern, at that period in America, with either decorativeness or technical polish, he knew that he had to discover a new dance product. He knew, or suspected, what dance could be in America, and he set out to make that vision a reality with his own body.

It was in Denver, 1911, that Ted Shawn first saw Ruth St. Denis dance. It was certainly love at first sight, but more than an attraction for a beautiful creature on stage, it was love for the kind of dance she represented. It was not classical ballet. It was not the popular social dances in which he was then so adept himself. Could it be religious dance? It was. This was something that he, from Middle America, did not know existed.

He saw prayers in dance form, ancient religious themes projected through dance. They were not, of course, Christian. But dedication, devoutness, service to God or gods were plainly present. In later years Shawn often said that he danced his way out of the church and into the theater, and St. Denis remarked that she had begun with theater and danced her way into the church. In passing, their careers and their lives met.

Shawn did not meet St. Denis in person at those Denver performances in March of 1911. But her performances gave him a vision of what dance could be. Dance, as an art form, was dead in America. From the vaudeville acts which came through Denver, from his voracious reading of periodicals as well as books, and from long talks with Hazel Wallack about her dancing at the Metropolitan Opera House and in other New York theaters, he knew this to be true. But what did he know about dancing?

He knew the ballet basics that Hazel Wallack had taught him: the ballet *barre*, adagio exercises, some leaps and turns (but not much of the "feet twitterings"). He was grateful to her for his first exposure to formal dance training. She used him as a partner in ballroom dance demonstrations. It was a pleasant, cozy, small-town relationship. It blossomed briefly into a romance and Ted gave Hazel an engagement ring.

But he soon outgrew the small-town opportunities, Hazel included. He had the restless urge to head for Los Angeles, and he was restive about the limitations of ballet. His own dance horizons had been broadened by movie travelogues. These, in the early days of movie shows, would have been classified under the general heading of "short subjects." Before the feature film, which rarely ran longer than ninety minutes before the advent of sound, audiences would get their two-hour money's worth with newsreels (all-important before the days of TV), a comedy short (cartoons came later), and a travelogue.

Young Ted went wild over the travelogues. As the camera recorded the customs and costumes of remote tribes and ancient nations, it paused briefly, tantalizingly so, to note strange dances. Ted devoured these snippets: a few measures of a Singhalese devil dancer in Ceylon, hulas in Hawaii, a stamp and an arrogant stance from Spain. Here he found men dancing and dancing as he felt men should dance, with strength and prowess and an awareness that they, in such ceremonials, were the stars, not the women. From these bits and pieces he patched together a technique of dance movement for men. He had moved out of the Denver limitations. Hazel knew it. She returned his ring. He turned to a new city, to a "travelogued" dance system, to a new life.

With his savings he went to Los Angeles. To earn a living he got a full-time job as a typist for the city's water department. He looked about for dance masters in what he had hoped would be the culture capital of America, but he could find none. Indeed, he felt that he knew as much about the art of the dance, and perhaps more, than any of the local teachers. With complete self-assurance, if not actual bravado, he hired a studio and began to teach. And as he taught others, he experimented with his new ideas and forms.

In looking about for possible studios and schools and instructors he had come across a Los Angeles teacher, Norma Gould, who had a school, a studio, pupils, and who was herself a dancer. Ted felt that she "would do." They talked it over. She kept her pupils in her own school and he kept his, but for exhibitions of social dances, they rehearsed themselves into the status of a team and used their pupils jointly for concerts in which Ted could try his hand at choreography, along with Norma.

Norma had, like Hazel Wallack, a ballet background, but she was in tune with Ted on choreographic experimentations and was eager to go beyond the confines of classical ballet. She was also adept at ballroom dances. A loose but fruitful partnership was established.

Ted went to the management of a hotel and suggested that they offer to the public "tango teas." These proved to be immediately successful. Norma and Ted would demonstrate the tango in its many variations and then separate to dance with the customers.

Ted, with the movie industry at hand, submitted scripts to the studios. Each script, of course, had a dance theme. All were rejected until at last *The Dance of the Ages* was finally accepted by the Thomas Alva Edison Company. In a handful of brief scenes Ted and Norma ranged from primitive man through classical Greek and courtly French to the current ballroom hits. Their students served as a corps. By today's standards it is pretty silly, but it was a film landmark in its day. Movie producers were not interested in dancing per se, but dance movements provided the camera with special challenges. In *The Dance of the Ages*, for example, bearded and learned ballet masters were gathered along the sides of a huge refectory table and, as they deplored the dances of the day, history unrolled before them while dancers, in miniature, performed on the table top. Ted's idea of a dance commentary seen in historic panorama was a valid one but Edison accepted it for a different reason: because of the opportunity it provided the camera to achieve striking effects—for those days—in juxtaposing full-size men and doll-like dancing Tom Thumbs.

The partnership of Shawn and Gould seemed solid. The tango teas were successful, the movie was made (in two weeks!), their separate dance classes grew steadily, but most important, they were building a repertory of exotic dances—which Ted evolved from the travelogues and avid reading of history—"esthetic" dances, numbers performed in nonballet movements to attractive music and, naturally, the social dances.

By 1914 they were ready to test their skills beyond Los Angeles. Ted had soon found that the West Coast had nothing to offer him that he didn't possess already. New York? Why not. He sold the Santa Fe Railroad a dance act for their employees—recreation series that would bring entertainment to the men and their families living along the line. Other performers had played this circuit of "reading" rooms. This kind of dancing seemed novel. Shawn and Gould, with assisting dancers (Adelaide Montgomery, Otis Williams) and musicians (soprano and pianist), were hired. The tour carried Ted Shawn eastward, without cost, as far as New York City and . . . Ruth St. Denis.

By the time that Ted Shawn met Ruth St. Denis, his personal characteristics, if not his character, and his artistic aims, if not his final focus, were evident. Are the molders of a man and a career environment? exposure? accident? necessity? Or does chronology have something to do with it? Heritage, that is.

Through his mother he traced the Booth family back to 1318 in England, although the name itself is of Danish origin. Shawn, who was knighted (the Order of Dannebrog) by the late King Frederik IX of Denmark in 1957 for his services in introducing stars of the Royal Danish Ballet to American audiences at the Jacob's Pillow Dance Festival, did some further tracking of the Booth family and came to the conclusion that his Booth forebears were among the Danish invaders of England at the time of King Canute. He was also delighted with the discovery that "the name 'Booth,' just as it does today means a sort of temporary shelter from which you sell something at a fair." (The Old Danish word is *both*.) Since most of his own life was spent in temporary quarters while selling his dance products around the world, this definition of "Booth" seemed to him to be most apt.

On his father's side he seems to have inherited his dictatorial characteristics along with a pioneering spirit and, by remote coincidence, his dashing romanticism. His grandfather, whose family name was von Schaun, fled the Germany of the Bismarck militaristic era along with other dissident Germans who settled in "colonies" in America. Grandfather von Schaun stopped in southern Indiana, married into the Ambrose family, and sired thirteen children, the youngest, Elmer Ellsworth Schaun, destined to become the father of another restless spirit, Ted Shawn. Father Schaun hated his name (he signed his name E. E. Schaun and as an author used the name E. Ellsworth Shawn), and he told his son how he came by it. He was named by two old maid sisters who recalled, with starry eyes, an episode that occurred at the close of the Civil War when their community of Carlisle, Indiana, was divided between Confederate and Union sympathizers. Into this little town came a contingent of Union soldiers. One saw that the local hotel-tavern was flying the Confederate flag. The proprietor was asked to take it down. He refused. The youthful warrior dashed into the hotel, up the stairs, out a dormer window, up a flagpole, and tore down the Confederate flag. The proprietor shot him dead. The spinsters floated along for years on this example of derring-do and asked von Schaun to name his youngest after this local hero, Lieutenant Elmer Ellsworth. Since he and his wife had already named a dozen offspring, he was relieved to have someone else take on the responsibility of naming the new baby. "So," reported Ted Shawn, "they named my father after this beautiful young man who had been shot to death in defense of his country. He was cursed with a dreadful name but blessed with the adventuresome spirit of a soldier."

When Elmer Ellsworth von Schaun was still a toddler, his parents died, and since his older brothers and sisters had either moved away or died—consumption, or today's tuberculosis, did away with several of them—he was reared by the family next door, the Arnolds, of English descent. "When my own father and my mother," Shawn wrote later, "who had been Mary Lee Booth, had their first child, my beloved brother who died so young, they named him Arnold. When I came along, they named me after our family doctor, Edwin

Myers. So there we both were, Arnold Booth Shawn and Edwin Myers Shawn, named after nonrelatives but after men who had been important in the past and in the present. Until his dying day I don't believe my father, who had legally changed his name from von Schaun to Shawn when he was twenty-one, realized that he had given his sons an Irish name (phonetically, at least!) in exchange for a German heritage."

Because Ted's father was a writer of stories as well as a reporter, stories were told at home. In speaking of his babyhood or, especially, his ancestry Ted in later years would say, "my father told me verbally that . . ." and then go on with his tale. Among the boy's favorites was how E. Ellsworth Shawn got his name. Mr. Shawn, whose short stories appeared in such national magazines as *McClure's* and *Century*, was a storyteller. Young Ted heard tales of his mother's side of the family not only from his mother but from his uncle, Galt Worthington Booth, and his wife, a chatty woman known to all as "Aunt Tad." He must certainly have been influenced by his story-spinning relatives.

Shawn, in his seventies, as do many old people, reminisced about the very distant past, about heritages. What had seemed of only passing interest to the boy took on significance for the man. He did admit that his mother's relationship to Edwin Booth was "partly legend[ary]," but later researches did indicate a distant connection. A family heritage which he made up (when he was about eighty) was intended for laughs, but there were undertones of the assumption of the messiah role in it when he said, "My grandmother's Me..e was Mary Porter, and my father's mother was Mary Ambro... mother was named Mary Lee Booth. There were three M... ancestry—I really should have been Jesus."

Aside from these heritages, the real and the adopted, ited, by blood lines, both practical inventiveness and ... tiveness. His maternal grandfather was one of the pio... telephone and telegraph industry in America. In fact, ... was this gentleman that he and Alexander Graham Bell ... traits on the same blue silk badge at major communicat... tions. Grandpa Booth also owned and operated the first telephone and telegraph companies in Indiana and Kentucky. One of his many employees was an ambitious young man named E. E. Shawn, whom he trained as a telegrapher. Before long the young man met the boss's daughter and married her.

Moving into the newspaper world was an easy step, for in those days, most newspapers had telegraph departments for the transmission of news. This was E. E. Shawn's job when he and his bride moved to Milwaukee where Arnold was born. The next move was to Kansas City where Ted was born and where E. E. held a post on the *Kansas City Star*. It was a logical step from transmitting news to writing it, and by the time the family had moved to Denver, E. E. was a leading editorial writer on the *Rocky Mountain News* and the *Denver Times*. In addition to these newspaper duties he found time to work as a free-lance writer of articles and stories. It was from him that Ted acquired his love of writing, eventually turning into a prolific writer of books, articles, and essays and an almost compulsive writer of letters.

But the Shawn family, so close and so loving, was breaking up. In 1903, when Ted was only eleven years old, both his mother and his only brother died (within eight months of each other). His love for his brother approached worship. "Arnold was everything I was not. He was a magnificent human being. When he died, at sixteen, he was six feet tall, weighed one hundred and sixty-five pounds topped by a magnificent head with bronze curls and a slightly aquiline nose. There was never any bickering or an unkind word between us. And he never indicated that he was ashamed of me because I didn't do the things that he did so well. He did everything superbly, and physically he was everything I was not. I was just a bookworm." Arnold died of spinal meningitis; his mother, after an abdominal operation.

At bedtime Ted would pretend to go to sleep, but as soon as his parents were certain that he had, he would make a tent out of his blanket, pull a lamp under it, and start to read a carefully concealed book. In the daytime he would hide a book underneath a bulky sweater and hie himself to a nearby field where sweet clover grew so high that it would conceal him. To the little boy it was like a forest where he had made his own pathways to his favorite hideaways always bringing book after book with him. (He once estimated that he had read five thousand books by the time he was fifteen.) Each day he took the four family membership cards to the library, took out four books and usually averaged reading four books a day. He was heedless of his mother's repeated admonition, "Teddy, you *must* exercise."

But the dancer-to-be, while admiring his brother's athleticism, his big and powerful muscles, his mastery of ice skating (when Teddy could barely stand up on wobbly ankles), did nothing about physical exercise—except to loathe it—until near tragedy, temporary paralysis, struck his own body some years later, in college. But even if he avoided sports, he never skirted any opportunity to show himself off in theatrical surroundings.

His mother, whom he loved deeply, provided him with constant exposure to the theater. He described her as "a very beautiful woman, majestic in her unusual height, five feet ten and one-half inches." Mrs. Shawn was not a Booth for nothing. She and Mr. Shawn, with press tickets available to them from the newspaper, attended the theater regularly. On her part Mrs. Shawn staged plays for schools and churches, and young Teddy acted in them. Even at home or at the Booth farm, where the families often visited, there were impromptu entertainments where an aunt, who had been a Gilbert and Sullivan star, would sing, an uncle strummed the guitar, and Teddy, without any training at all, would improvise dances, frequently on the Pierrot theme.

At home, in Kansas City, Missouri, he made good use of two rooms separated by sliding doors. One side became the stage, the other for the audience. Arnold was enlisted as stage manager and Teddy entertained. It was at this time, when he was almost six, that he solemnly had announced that he wanted to be a preacher on Wednesdays and Sundays and an actor the rest of the week. He said "actor" rather than "dancer" because dancing as a profession was not even known, let alone considered, in the Kansas City of the turn of the century. He did, as a child, have a few ballroom dance lessons, but he preferred the dancing that he made up and interwove with acting, playmaking, and, generally, showing off. Once, when he was going through a period of identifying himself with a young hero in a series of books for boys, he attended a party wearing an intensely uncomfortable and restricting collar, just as his hero would have worn. And when his mother pointed out that he would find it interfered with playing, he simply said, "But I want to look pretty."

All his life he would want to look pretty, although he grew up to be a handsome, virile man, not even a beautiful one like the Greek heroes and warriors he came to admire so much.

But in childhood the sense of theater was forever bubbling within him, and it exploded in all the amateur and at-home theatricals that he was associated with. Reading, writing, performing, and showing off—"I was a real brat," he recalled—were easily wedded to scholarship and an avid interest in learning. He was precocious. He entered high school at twelve, graduated at sixteen, entered the university the same year and would have been nineteen at graduation if diphtheria and paralysis and the ultimate call of the dance had not intervened.

His brother's death left him heartbroken and his mother's death soon after pressed heavily upon him, leaving him forlorn, rootless, deeply morose. Perhaps he even wondered if she had wished to follow Arnold. He and his father lived in boarding houses—the warmth of "home" was gone—and he was at first resentful when his father married again. He seemed much angrier at his father than at the woman he married, for he had known Mabel Walker all his life; she was a neighbor and often baby-sat with Teddy and Arnold when the Shawns were attending the theater. He never called her Mother and she never asked him to do so. She was always Mabel, as she had been when simply a dear family friend. Teddy the child and Ted the man liked her tremendously. She was not only sympathetic to his career but helped him out, even financially, whenever she could, long after his father had died. Mabel Shawn, in her own cool way, was very much a part of Ted Shawn's life. If she was cool by nature, Ted always felt that she was cold sexually and that she never provided his father with the physical love he needed. In this he sympathized deeply with his father. His own mother gone, the substitute mother seemed to supply dutifulness, friendship, but not the caressive love he himself sought.

In 1906 E. E. secured the writing job in Denver, and he and Mabel moved there, leaving Teddy with a young married couple who fed him well, treated him kindly, and looked out for him while he finished his high school year. Then, at sixteen, he joined his father and stepmother in Denver. Still mourning his mother and brother, he began to seek solace in the church. He had always been attracted to religion, especially when there was a touch of flamboyance about it. His mother had been an Episcopalian, but both she and her husband had transferred to the Presbyterian church when they moved from Milwaukee to Kansas City. Teddy was brought up in that church. But when he visited his aunt and uncle, Galt Worthington Booth and "Aunt Tad," in Kansas City, Kansas, across the river from home, he went with them to their Methodist church and met their young minister, Christian F. Riesner, who was destined to play, much later and in a different city, a major role in the life of Ted Shawn.

Teddy rediscovered him in Denver where, as Dr. Riesner, he had become minister of the Grace Methodist Church. At this point teenage Ted found not only the comfort and the security of faith which religion can provide but also an unexpected gateway to theater. Dr. Riesner, for his time, was very avant-garde. He put up a huge electric sign in front of his church; he used twenty-four sheet billboards, standard for theatrical enterprises, to advertise his church; he'd travel the neighborhoods shoving handbills, announcing his sermons, under front doors. His Sunday morning service was conventional Methodist, but the Sunday evening service was a cross between a refined concert and a vaudeville show, legitimatized by a ten-minute sermon. There would be the parables done in a Scottish dialect, a whistling soloist, performances by a mandolin or guitar club, appearances by Negro spiritual singers and the like. On one occasion the local florist supplied a free rosebud bearing a tag, "Grace Methodist Church, the Friendly Church," to everyone, and on another occasion the president of a mountain railroad line which crossed the Great Divide, contributed boxcars of snow with which the pulpit was packed from floor to ceiling to make an ecclesiastical winter wonderland.

It is small wonder that E. E. Shawn commented, "Chris Riesner is just a good circus manager gone wrong!" and later, when Dr. Riesner left Denver for New York City, he added, "That wasn't a call; that was a raise."

This dynamic man, possessed of the quality which a later generation would call charisma, took an interest in young Ted and asked him why he didn't move his pastoral "letter" from the Second Presbyterian Church to Grace Methodist. Ted hesitated. Then he blurted out, "Well, Dr. Riesner, dancing, card-playing, theater-going are cardinal sins in Methodist doctrine—I've seen it stated in writing. So how can I join your church? My parents and my brother and I played whist, we all attended the theater as often as possible, I even took social dance lessons when I was a child. I love dancing. So how can I become a Methodist?"

Riesner replied, "Well, if you can get up off your knees after praying to Jesus and, with a clear conscience, go to a dance or to the theater or play cards, I'll take you in to our church on the fact that your conscience is clear." Dr. Riesner, it turned out, was far more broadminded than college fraternity brothers and even the chancellor of the University of Denver, when Ted turned irrevocably to a life of dance. He probably would have found his pathway to dance even without the minister's approval, but this gentle linking of doctrine with theater, of the ecstasy of faith with the ecstasy of personal expression, led him in the years ahead to create many dances deeply rooted in the Christian religion, from his world-famous solo, *O Brother Sun and Sister Moon: A Study of St. Francis,* through the Protestant *Doxology* (known as Old Hundred) to an entire church service done in dance (1917, International Church, San Francisco).

Dr. Riesner was also of assistance in helping this strange, opinionated youth to continue his education. Before Teddy was to begin his senior year in high school, his father became ill with a disease which was characterized by extreme pain in the joints. He was unable to work, and Teddy was forced to get a job. His first was in an art store where he learned picture-framing in addition to serving as janitor for the shop. His salary was five dollars a week for a ten-hour day. Later he moved on to the art department of the Denver Dry Goods Company and became an expert in cutting glass, making mats, framing, gluing, nailing, and constructing shadow boxes.

On his father's temporary recovery (his disease was recurrent) and return to work, Teddy was able to go back to school. Dr. Riesner, through the generosity of a wealthy church member, was able to provide the lad with a tuition scholarship which enabled him to finish his high school education at the University of Denver Preparatory School (later called the Warren Academy), from which he was graduated in 1908. Immediately he entered the University of Denver itself and would have been eligible to graduate at nineteen if he had not missed a year of schooling. But as it turned out, he was never to graduate from college.

A career in dance, however, was by no means even contemplated at this time. When he was little and giving his performances at home with Arnold opening and closing the dining room doors, he settled for pantomimic tableaux: he'd strike a pose, announce "Highest Moon Sky," and Arnold would open the doors, let the onlookers savor the effect, and then close them. Teddy would change poses, announce "Sweethearts Dreaming," and the doors would open and shut. So it went.

By the time he became a member of the Grace Methodist Church, he was more active in his theatrics. One day, while Ted was entertaining friends in the lecture room of the church, where church suppers were often held, Dr. Riesner came in to see what the youngsters were up to and found Teddy singing and dancing "I'm the Yama-Yama Man." The reverend gentleman said not one word. He just looked and the proceedings came to a halt. But he never reproached Teddy. He was patient with what could only be termed excesses by Methodist standards, but he respected the boy's mind and his literacy. He even asked him to read proof with him on his first published book.

Teddy, of course, worked summers to earn money for books and other school necessities—twice he labored at a sawmill at an elevation of eight thousand feet in the Colorado mountains. He had received manual training in school in Kansas City, he had mastered the craft of picture-framing, he studied and practiced to become an expert typist, and at the university, he did his best to conform to the patterns of collegiate life, to get along with his fraternity brothers, and even to come to share their interests and their friendships.

Summer jobs opened up new areas of experience and touched off new and long-lasting friendships. Childhood and early adolescence without mother or brother was touched with sadness and morose solitude. But before paralysis and the exhausting battle for recovery had catapulted him into a wholly new life, the influences of Dr. Riesner and of the church, of rough and tough coworkers at sawmills, of dignified and socially acceptable college companions, of hymn sings by bonfire in the mountain nights, of formal education, and of occasional partying all threaded their ways into the fabric of a later life which was to be unorthodox, daring, even revolutionary by both artistic and moral standards. But in Denver in 1910 the inner rebellion, though dimly realized, had yet to explode.

3

As a child Teddy had liked being alone with his books and his thoughts and his dreams. Family and friends he needed as audiences for his impromptu theatricals. But as a university student Ted became gregarious and found a need to share his thoughts and his dreams with others. Companionship became essential to him. Two of his closest friends were Hugh Kellogg and Harold Hickey. They were, he later recalled, "an inseparable trio." Each had a bicycle and wherever they had spent an evening, they all started for their separate homes by accompanying each other, stopping for a long talk at each house, then deciding to see the next guy home and talking more there and moving on until the night was nearly spent.

It seemed like an enduring friendship, for they all had so much in common, endless things to talk about. They knew that their careers would be different—Ted, a minister; Hugh, a lawyer; Harold, a physician—but their high goals, though different, provided them with a stimulating unity. Yet in a very few years, when Ted had become a dancer and married St. Denis, a reunion in Denver launched with enthusiasm dwindled into reminiscences and a still later try, when Hugh and Harold had settled into family life, proved hopeless. Ted found that "life had seemed to take the color out of both of them. While not actually gray their whole personalities seemed gray. We just drifted apart because we never had anything but memories to talk about." What they thought of their one-time college friend is known only to themselves. Certainly they did not disapprove of his becoming a dancer. But what color did they find that Ted Shawn had become?

By this time insecurity had gone, at least on the surface, for self-doubts, fanned by his wife, would secretly haunt him all of his life.

29

As an adult he asserted, with considerable bravado, that he did things well, but as a child, an adolescent in Denver, he had no illusions about his own inadequacies. Of his brother he had said, "Arnold was everything I was not."

Arnold was the athlete, Teddy the bookworm. As Arnold glided across the ice, a superlative skater, Ted wobbled, his arms flailing like, as he put it, "a lame pelican trying to take off." He was unprepared, at this point, to surmount his physical inadequacies—he needed a greater challenge, desperation rather than discontent, to force him to become something more than an inept, adoring younger brother.

His adolescence, then, was gloomy, and he found himself in a psychological turmoil. Since he could not compete with his brother, what could he do? These inner uncertainties had something to do with heading him in the direction of the ministry of the church. If he couldn't do much with himself physically, perhaps he could do something for others. It was, he later said, a "messianic delusion," a desire to help mankind. His affection for the Methodist minister, Dr. Riesner, and the clergyman's interest in the strange youth, were certainly the final deciding factors in a decision stemming from athletic inferiority, bookishness, loneliness of the spirit if not in fact, and the curiously contradictory desire to dramatize everything.

His memory of his own moody, psychologically insecure adolescence made him patient with adolescents all his life. Arrogant and critical as he could be with adults, he was a softie with the young. He knew that many of their problems were silly, and he could be disapproving of youthful trends but he would say, "The only thing you can do for them is to love them. You can't criticize, you can't scold and you certainly mustn't say 'I know better.' Just love them. Hold them in your arms. Let them cry on your shoulder. Real love and sympathy will help them get through whatever they're suffering from, real or imagined. I know. I went through it."

His deep and genuine feeling for the young had much to do with his being referred to as "Papa Denishawn" when he was still young. St. Denis, considerably older, was never called "Mama Denishawn" by the members of the Denishawn company and the Denishawn students. She was always "Miss Ruth." After Denishawn had been dissolved, new Shawn students called him "Papa," and in his old age he always identified himself as "Papa" with every dancer he met, including some he had never met but simply corresponded with. His own childlessness simply increased his passionate concern with the well-being of the young.

Once when I was at Jacob's Pillow to do a review of a festival event, I saw a youth whom I recognized as that summer's station wagon driver for the Pillow's endless errands to nearby towns. He was pacing up and down the road, and I stopped my car to ask what was the matter. "I wrecked the station wagon," he said. "I think I was driving all right, maybe a little fast, but then I had an accident. No one was hurt but the car's a mess and I'll get fired and I don't know what to do." I gave him advice: "Run into Shawn's office—in tears, if you can manage it—and throw yourself at his feet and say, 'I've done something awful and I don't know what to do or say and I don't know what you'll do with me but I had to come right to you.'" (P.S. He was not fired and he continued to drive for the rest of the summer.)

Methodism did not dampen young Ted's ardor for theater. He had convinced Dr. Riesner that for him at least dancing was not antithetical to religion, but the established church and the Methodist-dominated university held other views. Somehow plays were all right and skits and staged songs, but social dancing was taboo. Since ballroom dance was all that Ted knew, other than the fanciful living room capers he had devised as a child, he wanted to engage in social dance. Since that activity was banned on campus and since his fraternity brothers wanted to hold dances, Ted came up with invitations worded thusly: "You're invited to come and play folk games with us to music on a slick floor." It worked.

The splitting of theological hairs infuriated and amused Ted. Dr. Riesner had privately approved of Ted's justification of his personal linking of Christian behavior and theater, although he did not approve of it in principle. Years later, when Riesner was preaching in New York City and Ted gave a dance recital at Town Hall, the minister attended even though he knew that his former charge would be dancing the Twenty-third Psalm. Afterward he said, "Ted, that was a stronger and better sermon than I have ever preached." Forthwith he invited him to come to his own church and, on a Sunday night, preach from his own pulpit on the text from the Psalms, "Praise ye the Lord in the dance." Ted looked at the congregation, noting many stern-lipped elders present, and said, "You believe in the Bible. It is not to be interpreted allegorically. It is explicit and you must believe in it as it is worded. Now here is a clear, curt, concise command, 'Praise ye the Lord in the dance.' Have you done so today? Then if not you have committed a sin of omission." One of the congregation rose and shouted, "Amen, brother!"

But this was not Denver, 1909. The university's chancellor, Dr. Buchtel, would attend one-act plays and skits, sit in the front row, and smile benignly at Ted, assuring him that he had talent. Yet barely more than a year later when Ted, recovering from a near disastrous illness, left the university and danced in public with his new partner, that same chancellor, as noted, had told the young man that he was sorry that he had resigned because he would have relished the opportunity to expel him.

But Ted, emerging from his adolescent doldrums, managed to reconcile church and approved college studies with theatrics of all sorts and the beginnings of body discipline, first through accepted labors and then through incipient dance.

At the university he was thrown into close company with a girl named Allene Seaman, whose fine mind and advanced views on social structures and ethics fascinated Ted. She was a senior and he a freshman, but they were in the same Greek class. Both lived in town and both had to take the forty-five-minute trolley-car journey daily to the university, so they rode together. The Greek class was small—only six—which meant frequent translation recitings for each pupil, and since one, when called on, always said "unprepared," that left a hard-worked group of five. Allene and Ted soon detected the teacher's pattern of calling on the students so they divided the prescribed translation in half, one doing one part and the other responsible for the remainder, and during the streetcar ride there was a quick exchange of translations so that each would know the total gist of the assignment while praying to be called upon for his or her special area of concentration.

The Greek arrangement with Allene worked out well enough but it did more by bringing him into contact with a person with, for those times, fairly radical connections. Summers she spent in East Aurora, New York, where her connections included a close friendship with the philosopher Elbert Hubbard, who did such questionable things as giving jobs to ex-convicts or to anyone else ostracized from society and making such breezy comments as, "Often a man's whole reputation depends upon his suspenders not breaking." Allene, long before women's lib was dreamed of, was active in feminist causes and created more than one stir on campus. This led to a play which Ted wrote and, with fellow students, produced.

The play, called *The Female of the Species*, was inspired by Allene but presented after her graduation and departure to East Aurora. Ted's story was about a girl such as Allene who took the soapbox for women's rights so continuously that her sorority sisters and Ted's fraternity brothers decided to teach her a lesson. In the play the students convinced the girl that they had given her a sleeping potion, and that like Rip Van Winkle she had slept for twenty years. To convince her of this, after she had gone to sleep, they scurried about and changed everything in the room. She awoke to a completely woman-dominated country: woman mayor, woman governor, woman president of the nation.

Ted sent Allene a manuscript of the farce, and she replied that the program left her "furiously curious" and that the plan of the play simply proved that Ted was "popping with ideas" just as he was when she had first met him.

The near sedentary adolescence also came to an early end with Ted's job in the logging camp. There were eighty men, all of them stalwarts, besides Ted, who had never done anything physically strenuous before. He recalled that he was "as soft, in body, muscle and skin, as a girl." His stepmother, as she saw him off on the train, said, "Well, you'll be back soon." But he stuck it out at ten hours a day for wages of $2.50 a day. Teddy, accustomed to homelife, found living in a verminous bunkhouse a ghastly experience and the food even ghastlier. But with the arrival of a new chief engineer, things started to look up. He was a "gentle" man in Ted's eyes, and he and his family lived in tents rather than in the bunkhouse. These new friends, Mr. and Mrs. Gillette and their son (a year younger than Ted) and daughter (a year older), had been Salvation Army captains, and they took an interest in Ted and another young Denver logger who was the son of a minister. All were drawn together by religious leanings and by attachment to family living.

Mrs. Gillette, buxom and good-natured, fed them well, and at night, under the clear, starry Colorado skies, with the mountains soaring around them, they lit bonfires and sang revival hymns.

Ted had a new family. He and the Gillette son Paul made a lasting friendship which, through correspondence, continued a lifetime. Another brother, whom he never met, was at that time imprisoned in New York on a charge of murder. He had been convicted at the first trial, his family labored at the logging camp and elsewhere to pay for an appeal and new trial, but their son was executed. Ted's interest in this distant tragedy was that the imprisoned brother, Chester, and his case served Theodore Dreiser for his famous novel *An American Tragedy*. Whether this was generally known or not is uncertain. Ted simply wrote, "I was in on this."

There were two work summers at the logging camp separated by a summer of less taxing work at Estes Park in northern Colorado. Here Ted was a delivery boy working for a smart business woman, Elizabeth Foote, who had worked her way up from salesgirl to buyer in a Denver dry goods company and had bought a general store in Estes Park. Ted's job was to curry and care for the horse that pulled the delivery wagon and to make daily trips along the winding mountain roads with a load of produce ranging from high-grade candy and a yard of handmade lace to one-hundred-pound cakes of ice and rented sewing machines.

To amuse himself on his trips he'd sing hymns full voice, although his singing voice was not and never became even adequate. Still, at the Denver Preparatory School, he had taken some singing lessons because he had fallen briefly in love with a girl who was planning a singing career, and he had even sung two solos, "A Son of the Desert Am I" and "Boys Will Be Boys," on the graduating programs, but his Estes Park horse was always to remain his most sympathetic listener.

The chief influence at Estes was Miss Foote herself. She was active in a religious movement called Divine Science, which Shawn later described as a "split-off" from Christian Science. She knew that her young friend was studying for the ministry and that since his training was centered in the Iliff School of Theology on campus, a Methodist-dominated school, her religious approach would be antithetical to his courses. She said as much, but he replied that if he could be upset by other religious ideas he should face it now and come to grips with them. He even said that if he was tempted by conversion he would not stick with Methodist teachings. "I cannot preach anything I cannot defend," he declared.

Delicately and sensitively Miss Foote explained to the boy her metaphysical beliefs. They impressed him, even if they did not wholly win him. He reported his talks to Dr. Riesner, who said bluntly, in the face of a rebellion against orthodox teachings, "She is a wicked woman." Yet Dr. Riesner came more and more to accept young Ted's unorthodoxies through dance, and Shawn himself later noted that his long conversations with Miss Foote—centering on "There is neither life, truth, substance, nor intelligence in matter. All is infinite mind and its infinite manifestations"—prepared him for his life with St. Denis, a very ardent but unorthodox Christian Scientist who "swooped off into Buddhism, Zoroastrianism, and so on" all her life.

These were the university years. The religious drive was exploring, developing, balancing "isms." An awareness of physicality came to a sedentary youth. Friendships were forged. That "divine discontent" which Martha Graham would treat as a philosophical truth a half century later was present in him and in his ambitions, which thrust him toward both pulpit and theater. The decision was made for him, at least in part, by the almost disastrous attack of diphtheria which, while immobilizing his body, mobilized his mind into setting a lifetime course of action. Lying in a hospital bed he began to think. He began, curiously enough, to dance.

4

Diphtheria struck suddenly, almost fatally. It was Ted's junior year at the university. He was rushed to Steele Hospital, a center for contagious diseases, and remained there for many weeks, almost in solitude. Briefly he shared a room with a lad from Colorado Springs, but for the most part he was in a private room from which family and friends were barred. The case was severe—a gland swelled to the size of a grapefruit, he felt as if his throat were laced with "ribbons," he was fed through a tube and required to keep his head motionless on the pillow. A new antitoxin was used, perhaps in an overdose, and although it saved his life, it left him paralyzed from the waist down.

He could not move, he was in pain, but he found that, alone, he had never before thought so clearly. Indeed, that was all he could do, think, and that, he later remarked, was "just about the most dangerous thing you can do, think."

He thought and it occurred to him that he had never really thought before. He had read voraciously and listened attentively and had believed pretty much what he was told. There had been fleeting doubts but he had been so busy learning that he had done little questioning. Certainly he had not questioned himself. He had been fed by his parents, his minister, his teachers, his friends. Now when he couldn't eat or move, he decided to clean his mental house with thought. Brashly he decided he would toss out everything he had learned and start all over, putting into his mind only those things he had proved to his own satisfaction, at least, to be true. Naturally he found that some past instructions stuck and that he was not enough of a scientist to prove that everything he wanted to believe in was the truth, but one thing he did, while lying there, was to think himself right out of the church, especially the Methodist Church (but not religion) and right into the theater.

He couldn't do much about the theater at first. When he was no longer a danger to others, he was dismissed from the hospital and sent home, unable yet to move. He just lay there and decided that he had to begin somewhere. Every ounce of will power he had was channeled into trying to wiggle a single toe. Once he had mastered the toe, the next major project was planned: to flex a foot. Weary, painful days passed, and then a knee began to bend.

Finally the moment of great drama arrived, when Ted swung his legs over the side of the bed and, clutching the posts, pulled himself to a standing position. He couldn't walk but he could stand. Standing would be all right for a preacher, but not for an actor. And an actor he thought he would be. A dancer? Not yet.

He kept at the exercises, self-prescribed, until he could walk. It was a clumsy, lurching walk, uncertain in direction, tentative in balance.

This Promethean conquest of his own infirmities made him more deeply aware of the wonder, the beauty of the body itself. As a child he had avoided exercise and that body mastery which most sports require, but he had marveled at his brother's physical beauty and at his prowess in everything he demanded of his body.

His focusing upon muscular development and controls was at first, of course, therapeutic. But once repairs had been achieved, enhancements of the body quite naturally followed. (For myself I know that as a child I hated calisthenics and any sports other than swimming and horseback riding. I even managed to coerce the family doctor into saying that I might possibly have indications of heart murmurs so that I could get out of taking gym. But once in college I did a swift switch and not only took the required calisthenics but also moonlighted, and answered roll call, for other boys who preferred to skip it, so that I was doing two gym classes a day and even learning to wrestle. When I took my first dance class, I was ready for aiming at a strong, handsome body.)

Ted Shawn, a generation before, had made the same discoveries. They influenced him all his life. When he had weight problems—a continuing concern—he would live on hamburger and lettuce until the pounds peeled off. I remember having lunch with him in the

1930s in Boston at a funny, attractive little place called the Toby
House, when he was dieting. He ate his hamburger and lettuce, and
when it came dessert time, he said to me, *"You're* having Indian
pudding. It's a specialty here." I replied that I disliked Indian pudding. He ordered it for me. When it arrived, he took his own tea-
spoon, scooped up an infinitesimal bit of pudding with a tiny dollop
of whipped cream, put it in his mouth, rolled his eyes heavenward
and sighed in absolute ecstasy. (He would not give up cocktails for
diets, however, because he insisted that water, unless it came from
the old farm well at Jacob's Pillow, was "an abomination.")

The state of the body, especially his own, became almost an ob-
session with him. Some of it was genuinely esthetic. He loved the
Greek ideal of nudity, of youths at the ancient Olympics, entering
races and wrestling matches with gleaming, oiled, nude bodies. He
wrote a chapter on nudity and dance in one of his early books, *The
American Ballet*, and also early in his career he vowed he would dance
nude in public, which he ultimately did, with the exception of a
stylized figleaf, in his *Death of Adonis* (1923), a solo in which body,
headcurls, and figleaf, were "marbleized" to resemble a statue.

At Jacob's Pillow, headquarters for his company of Men Dancers in
the 1930s, he would read aloud to the dancers and male students (all
nude) on a sun-bathed terrace during lunch hours. I also remember
his saying that if every human, male and female, were required by
law to stand nude for one hour once a year on his village green or
city hall plaza, there would be no obesity, no flabbiness, perhaps no
debauchery. Vanity would take care of that!

Vanity, perhaps, explained why he liked to have nudes taken of
himself until he was eighty. At least once a year, I would get a
snapshot of him, either nude or partly covered by a branch, a leaf
(or a hibiscus), and on the back, in his very neat writing, "Not bad
for . . ." whatever the age was.

Aside from the genuine belief in the esthetic of nudity and his personal vanity there was, very possibly, a recurring act of celebration
of thanksgiving while he recorded, as much for himself as for others,
the proof of regeneration in a body once paralyzed so long ago in
Denver . . .

The school year was too far along for him to catch up, but time
was not to be wasted. The superintendent of the Sunday school at

the Grace Methodist Church ran a business school with his brother, and the two offered the convalescent a free course in typing, shorthand, bookkeeping. The practical side of the boy jumped at the chance of learning a skill that would, if worse came to worst, keep him employed. But how to get to school when he could barely walk? A neighborhood girl, Winifred Boynton, decided she would take the business course too, perhaps because she was attracted to the handsome, somewhat helpless young man. She owned an electric car, and each morning, after Ted had struggled into his clothes and made his slow descent of the stairs, she would drive him to school. She was too considerate of his manliness to help him up the stairway to the second-floor classroom, but she kept close to his elbow just in case. In the afternoon the pattern was simply reversed.

When the course was completed, Ted landed a job quickly but soon moved to a position with the Northwestern Mutual Life Insurance in Denver, a position he held until he left for Los Angeles and the start of his meteoric career. But in Denver, in addition to his clerical duties, he became friendly with young people in a little theater group and, in order to improve his physical state through more demanding exercise, enrolled in a ballet class. Friends and family, knowing he hated sports, suggested ballet studies with Hazel Wallack because such exercise would not only help bring back his body but, as they expressed it, give him "an expressive use" of his body.

Hazel, though very young (not much older than the eighteen-year-old Ted), had already had a brief career in the ballet at the Metropolitan Opera House in New York and had been a pupil of the Met's first prima ballerina, Malvina Cavallazzi, who had danced in 1883 at the Met's opening season and headed the Met school in 1909. Since Madame Cavallazzi had been regarded in her native Milan, in London, and in New York as a major ballerina (even though she specialized in male roles done *en travesti*), one may be certain that Hazel Wallack had received superior training. Certainly it is incontrovertible that she helped Ted enormously not only through carefully selected ballet exercises but also professionally. Indeed, after painful months of body rehabilitation under Hazel's tutelage Ted Shawn made his professional dance debut as the tall and very handsome partner of the tall and very attractive Hazel.

Ted, scrupulous about money matters throughout his long career, did not permit anyone to give him anything. His job with the insurance company paid for his ballet lessons and an extra job—three hours every evening and six hours every Sunday at the Denver Public Library—made it possible for him to meet all bills. In his newfound enthusiasm for ballet, he'd get up each morning a little after six and in his bedroom do a ballet *barre* sequence of exercises, holding onto the bedpost in lieu of a proper classroom *barre*, plus adagio, or slow ballet stretch, and balance exercises he could do in a small room.

Hazel, in need of a partner to match her professional standards and, particularly, her height, pushed Ted in the daily classes after his working hours and in rehearsals after he finished his library stint at nine in the evening. For the Wallack performances, he partnered her in classical ballet numbers but was especially impressive in exhibition ballroom dances, which were coming into increasing popularity from coast to coast. Hazel had brought some of the popular favorites with her, and one was *French Love Waltz*, the number in which she wore a slit skirt which, inescapably and intentionally, exposed her leg as she slid gently into a graceful semikneel. It was this position, photographed for the Denver paper (and incidentally for posterity), which aroused Chancellor Buchtel's ire to such a pitch that he had blurted out the scathing comment that he wished Ted were still a university student so that he could have the pleasure of expelling him. Shawn told and retold the story gleefully for the next sixty-two years.

He also enjoyed telling and retelling his fraternity brother's comment, "Ted, *men* don't dance," and that his rejoinder about the great males of the Russian ballet and the dances of men in almost every culture was always met with "that's all right for Russians and pagans but not for Americans."

Although Ted and Hazel became "loosely engaged" as he described it later, she represented, professionally at least, only a stepping stone in his career. He had the urge to travel, see more and be seen more. Hazel had left a promising career in New York because of her mother's health and need of the clear Colorado climate. Ted wanted to move on both geographically and in terms of dance range. Hazel was all ballet. Even the dances she composed on national folk themes or classical Greek subjects were all couched in classical ballet. Ted knew, even before Hazel came into his life, that there was more to the world of dance than just ballet. As a schoolboy he had earned after-school money delivering papers, and one of his customers was the manager of the local Pantages Theater, that chain which supplied vaudeville to the country. The manager let Teddy stand in the back of the house and catch an act or two almost every day.

In vaudeville he was particularly struck with a female impersonator named Lind who included a good deal of dancing in his act. When Shawn was older and a successful dancer himself, he looked back and recognized that one of Lind's dances had been derived from Maude Allan's celebrated dance shocker *Salome* and that he must also have been an accomplished Spanish dancer.

By the time he was working for the insurance company, movies were pushing back vaudeville but broadening the dance experience of the young man. For his lunch hour, he'd dash to the movies, nibbling cashew nuts and fudge squares, and watch a Pathé newsreel with, if luck were with him, a heady glimpse of the newest dance craze in New York, a tango teaser, or something as exotic as a few frames of a wild primitive dance in a travelogue.

He was shrewd enough to know that even though he had recovered from the paralysis, he was not young enough and agile enough to become a *premier danseur*, and Ted would not have been satisfied with being a *corps de ballet* dancer or even a soloist in a ballet troupe or even a ballet bigshot in Denver. If he could not become a *premier danseur*, he would become a *premier* of some other sort—because he had to be first.

But what could he do with a background of about two years of ballet, admiration for a female impersonator, glimpses of dancing in newsreels, and his still unchanged boyhood desire to go on stage, show off, and "look pretty"? All this would at best lead to self-indulgent dilettantism, and he had much too good a mind to settle for that. The catalytic agent that united his inadequate background with his lofty ambitions was a woman, Ruth St. Denis, and the agent worked its chemistry simply at that first sight of her in Denver in 1911. Ruth St. Denis, a professional dancer for fifteen years and an international star for five, performed *The Incense*. Teddy watched.

He marveled. It was like a religious conversion. It changed his whole life.

Until that performance he had suffered from what he called "a split consciousness." He had left the church for the theater. He had left religion for the dance. When he saw *The Incense* he knew that they were one. He had been dimly aware that if one pursues the dance upstream toward its source, he will come to religion and if, in parallel fashion, one pursues religion to its earliest manifestation of celebration, he will find dance. He only sensed this when he saw St. Denis, and he could not quite put it into the words that he would discover some years later in Havelock Ellis's *The Dance of Life*, a book St. Denis often referred to as the dancer's Bible. Ellis wrote: "If we are indifferent to the art of dancing, we have failed to understand not merely the supreme manifestation of physical life, but also the supreme symbol of spiritual life."

Just what had he seen in *The Incense?* This was the first dance on the first program that Ruth St. Denis had presented before a startled audience at New York's Hudson Theater in 1906. Since then it, and her other Oriental dances of mystical nature, dramatically staged, had strongly influenced the course of dance and even of the theater in America and in Europe. There was nothing authentic in step or gesture in her East Indian dances—the word "ethnic" would not be used to describe the authentic dances of a given culture for another half century—yet she had captured the spirit of a people who had danced their religion for two thousand years.

For *The Incense*, the curtain rose on a dimly lit stage. It was not quite dawn. The back curtains parted and a single figure came through. She bore in her hand a tray of embers and incense, and with these she offered prayers to the gods for the well-being of her household for another day. As she crumbled the incense on her tray or on two stands at either side of the stage, the smoke rose delicately, almost wispily, heavenward bearing her silent prayers. And as the smoke spiraled, her own arms mirrored the pattern in ripples which coursed delicately from shoulders to fingertips as the body swayed almost imperceptibly matching the thread of smoke curving upward. First one arm would reflect the smoke spirals as it dropped incense in the coals, and then the other arm, and near the peak of her dance she placed the tray on the floor, and both arms rippled as if they were not of flesh and bone but as evanescent as smoke. Quietly she picked up her tray, moved backward through the curtain, and disappeared. This was *The Incense*, the dance which changed the life of Ted Shawn.

While Teddy was still a schoolboy, Ruth St. Denis was making history. She had been born in 1877 and raised on a New Jersey farm by a remarkable mother, one of the first licensed women doctors in the United States, who had given up medicine for divine healing, and a brilliant but improvident father who invented things and occasionally drank too much. Ruthie Dennis was precocious. At five she dashed into the spotlight at a barn dance, at nine she acted out the Crucifixion (and nearly did away with herself) in order to identify with it, at twelve she sat in the old apple tree and read Mary Baker Eddy's *Science and Health*, Kant's *Critique of Pure Reason*, and Dumas's *Camille* (the kind of unique mélange she pursued for the rest of her life), and from her mother she learned something of the movement principles of François Delsarte (a scientist of movement who was to prove to be another link between her and Shawn).

There were some dancing lessons, but mainly it was a very agile body and a natural instinct for theater which made Ruthie Dennis a dancer. At first she did not link up religion and Delsarte exercises with dancing. She enjoyed moving, and she became at about sixteen, give or take a year or two, a professional dancer in a variety show. She was admired for her high kicks, splits, and rollovers and was proud to her dying day that her kicks had been unusual in that her leg did not simply snap up and back but rose ear-high and descended slowly. Her first job earned her twenty dollars a week for eleven shows a day. After four or five years of this, including a few ballet lessons she hated, she was spotted by the great director-impresario-producer-actor, David Belasco, who "canonized" her into St. Denis. For five years she played in his productions, usually as an actress who did some incidental dancing and singing. She was busy as a minor performer in plays starring the popular Mrs. Leslie Carter.

In 1899 in London two American girls, destined for greatness but still only minor players in show business, were performing. Isadora Duncan, in a production of Shakespeare's *A Midsummer Night's*

Dream, earned a review in the *Stage* magazine: "Five of the attendant fairies are prettily played by Miss Isadora Duncan. . . ." In a later issue, a report on *Zaza*, starring Mrs. Leslie Carter, simply noted: "Miss Ruth Dennis as Adele." In a very few years Isadora would be dancing the great symphonies, launching single-handedly an explosive restoration of the art of dancing to the glory it enjoyed in classical Greece. And Ruth St. Denis would be dancing, heretically, about God, dancing, heretically, with the rhythms of the breath and not the beat of the feet. Both would lay the foundations of twentieth-century dance for generations to come.

When Shawn was an old man, I wrote a monograph, or treatise, for *Dance Perspectives* magazine called "The Legacy of Isadora Duncan and Ruth St. Denis." In it a quote from Martha Graham stated that our dance had been born of this dual matriarchy. Ted Shawn, reading it, was furious with me. Rather pitifully he said, "You know I had something to do with the dance in America. I'm the father." I tried to explain to him that I was writing about his predecessors and not about him except in conjunction with Miss Ruth and that a treatise centered upon his contributions would treat her only peripherally. This did not mollify him, but his anger represented the personal cross he chose to bear all of his professional life, the burden of being St. Denis's younger husband.

Intellectually he would have to admit that she had made history before he had even commenced to dance and that she had created enduring masterpieces of theater dance and, equally, that Duncan had made an imprint on dance that would never fade. But his Prussian, male ego could not accept fact. It wasn't helped when Miss Ruth said—and it spread—"Teddy will never be happy until he admits to himself—he need not say it out loud—that of the two I am the greater." The St. Denis ego was absolutely secure, the Shawn ego was not. But in 1911 there was only adoration of St. Denis—a half century of aching jealousy was yet to come.

St. Denis, after the not very memorable 1899 season in London, returned to America for more Belasco tours. It was on one of these, in Buffalo, New York, that she saw a commonplace object which grabbed her mind, triggered her imagination, altered her life, and affected the world's theater. It was 1904. The object was a poster advertising Egyptian Deities cigarettes. It showed a seated Isis flanked by Egyptian columns. She was serene, mysterious, ageless. St. Denis was with a good friend and Belasco actress, Honoria Donner (whom Ruth called Patsy), having a snack in a dreary restaurant on a rainy night when she glanced up and saw the poster. She was hypnotized.

Back at the rooming house she fretted and said to her friend, "Patsy, I must have that poster. Go and get it." She never knew why she couldn't get it herself, but she was almost in a state of shock, and Patsy Donner did as she was bidden. The poster went on tour and was propped up against a series of hotel beds from Buffalo to San Francisco. Along the way Ruthie visited every museum she could find and asked to see any Egyptian artifacts, no matter how skimpy the collection. She filled Patsy Donner with her ideas. She wrote Mother St. Denis. She couldn't wait for the tour to end. She would leave Belasco and the show business world she knew. To Patsy she said, "You know I'm not going to be just an Egyptian dancer. I'm going to be Egypt!" Not for Ruth St. Denis, the Little Egypt belly dancers of expositions and carnivals. She would be a whole nation and its culture.

Patsy, devoted to Ruth, helped her and stood by her after she left Belasco in 1904 until 1906 when she earned almost nothing—except for a few performances at high society parties—while exploring her new world of dance. Mother St. Denis was a continuing force behind Ruth's career and life and would remain the believer, the promoter, and the disciplinarian for a decade, until Ted Shawn came along to sweep Ruthie away, making Mother obsolete.

Ruth's brother, whom his parents never got around to naming, was simply called "Brother" and signed himself B. St. Denis until he died in his eighties, a few years after his sister died at ninety-one (or ninety-two or ninety-three). Brother was a geologist-scholar and also something of an inventor, a bent he inherited from their inventor-father. For her new concept of theater Ruthie needed elaborate lighting effects. Some she asked for did not exist. Brother invented the devices to make them possible. For controlled overhead lighting he himself sat in a basket-cage hauled by pulleys high above the proscenium, and with manual electrical extensions threw a light on his sister, when she was playing a goddess, from above.

"Buzz," as he was called by the family, also doubled as an extra for St. Denis's Oriental ballets and performed a great samurai duel with her in her Japanese dance drama, *O-Mika*. B. St. Denis was very important, in those first years of experimentation, to Ruth St. Denis.

The amazing thing, when she came to do the long-postponed *Egypta* in 1910, after she had won international fame, was that she did indeed do a work which was not only a day in the life of Egypt but the life of the nation itself, starting with dawn, with prayer, with the river Nile (she was the river itself), with the labors of the working people of Egypt, with temple ceremonies, with entertainment of the pharaoh, and with the final judgment when, before the god Osiris, the heart of Egypt is weighed against the feather of truth. In the ballet the heart balanced, symbolizing a pure heart, and the figure of Egypt, Egypta, guided by Ra, moved on to the next world. It was a monumental concept for theater let alone for dance and it was generated by a cigarette poster.

Egypta did not come first simply because St. Denis could not afford to stage it during the two years when she planned her new life and her new theater dance. The whole St. Denis family rallied to her support while she worked, studied, tested, and found her new pathway. She created *The Incense*, then *The Cobras*, the dance of an East Indian beggar woman, a snake charmer. Her two arms were the cobras, and from four hatpins headed with bright green stones Father St. Denis fashioned rings which became the cobras' malevolent eyes. So effective was this dance that it was imitated by massed "cobra girls" in vaudeville. Her ballet *Radha* had to come before *Egypta* because of lower production expense, but it proved to be a keystone in her career.

Ruthie knew about East Indian temple dance only what she could read in the *Encyclopaedia Britannica* and what she saw at an East Indian village reproduction at Coney Island. She fashioned a work which, she later happily admitted, was about a Hindu goddess dancing a Buddhist concept in a Jain temple. But she had captured the spirit of Indian religious dance to such a degree that when she and Ted and their Denishawners made a triumphant tour of India twenty years later, the St. Denis Indian dances actually instigated a renascence of India's then decaying dance. Books in classical Sanskrit report on St. Denis's deep and lasting impact on the ancient dance of

India. This was the genius that young Ted had seen. This was the woman whose dancing resolved for him instantly any conflict between church and theater.

Shortly after arriving in Los Angeles he had two evening classes daily and, ambitious to try out his choreographic ideas, he selected his best pupils and formed a little group. "I knew more about dance than any other teacher to be found," he said. "Egotistic but an actual fact." The working relationship was established with Norma Gould, who specialized in children's classes rather than in young adults. Norma would serve his purposes for two years as Hazel had done for the preceding two.

With the water company, Ted had a nine-to-five job, but with the ballroom dance craze sweeping the nation—*thé dansants* and tango teas were mushrooming everywhere, Ted was determined to capitalize on the fad. Maurice, in New York, had been the foremost proponent of the tango; the Castles, Vernon and Irene, were on their way to becoming the most famous dancers in America. Ted continued to learn steps from magazine articles and newspaper features, from movie newsreels and movie specials on social dancing. He even latched onto any traveler from the East Coast and said, "Show me what they're doing."

He got a job for himself and Norma first at the Hotel Angelus and introduced the tango teas to the city. He asked his water department boss if he could take only fifteen minutes for lunch, and leave work at four fifteen. The boss, already amazed at Ted's energy, said yes, so the boy had a chocolate milk shake with raw egg for lunch and at four fifteen dashed off to meet Norma for their tango stint. They demonstrated for large gatherings and once they had done all the new dances, they separated and Norma danced with the men and Ted with the ladies, instructing them in the new steps, the tango, the maxixe, the lulu fado, and other dances. Norma and Ted wore ballroom dress both for their exhibitions and the instructional minglings. After the tango tea, Ted would race off to his studio and teach two classes in a row. Then there would be rehearsals of new choreography. And if that were not enough, Ted then arranged for exhibitions at the foremost hotel in town, the Alexandria, from eleven until midnight. He'd be at work the next morning at nine.

He and Norma and the little dance company also had club dates to perform and that too augmented the income. Then came *The Dance of the Ages* movie (providing two weeks of salaries) which, though the script was conceived by Ted, was a co-choreographic enterprise involving Norma as well.

Ted, of course, knew nothing about ancient Egyptian or Greek or Roman dances, but he knew as much about them as anyone else in Los Angeles, so he just made up dances that he thought would be right. A Broadway trade paper's Los Angeles section reviewed it as "different from any photoplay you have ever seen, an Edison feature extraordinary." It was on a bill with four reels of comedy, and the reviewer promised the audience "two hours of laughs." The Edison studios were in Long Beach, so Ted, Norma, and their cast commuted daily in order to get back to the city for evening classes.

Shortly after the film was finished, Ted came across an article, "The Making of the Personality," by the Canadian-born poet, Bliss Carman. Among other things, Carman wrote about dance in such a way that Ted was transfixed with excitement. Some of his own images were in the writings, some questions were almost answered. Here indeed was a cultured being, a man of taste and sensitivity, a poet. He wrote to him asking where he could study such a way of dance if there was such a place or did it exist only in theory? Carman wrote back yes, and told him that the person to study with was Mrs. Mary Perry King who lived in New Canaan, Connecticut. She was exploring rhythmic movement possibilities related to drama, to movement supported not by instrumental music or song but by the spoken word. Carman had actually written rhythmic dramas for her, including one called *Daughters of Dawn*.

Ted felt he must go east for studies. But how? He had saved about three thousand dollars. Then he learned about the Santa Fe Railroad's program for its employees, of entertainers, traveling across the country. The company paid its entertainers no fees but gave them a round trip to New York and back. Ted talked Norma into it. For Ted it turned out to be a one-way passage.

Billed as "interpretive" dancers they offered some "à la" dances, à la Grecque, à la Hongrois, and so on, in addition to the popular ballroom dances, the Castle Walk among them.

They played Needles, Gallup, Amarillo, Chillicothe, and places in between, before and after, coast to coast. Their stages were usually inadequate, and improvised dressing rooms ranged from empty swimming pools to unused billiard parlors. The Pullman accommodations, including food, were first-rate, and the workers and their families seemed to enjoy the show. They hit New York on a bitter cold winter morning, at six o'clock, in 1913. The first thing Ted did was to hop an open-top Fifth Avenue bus and do the entire route, up and back.

Next stop, New Canaan.

Mrs. King, very plump and ringleted, taught eight hours a day six days a week. Ted didn't know at the time that she had been a pupil of Mrs. Richard Hovey, a superb exponent of the principles of the French scientist of movement, François Delsarte, for she never gave Delsarte any credit, and Ted, at that time, had not even heard of Delsarte. Mrs. King went about her rhythmic business to the point of having her pupils wear shoes with curved soles, rather like rockers, that were supposed to give the individual a more perfect rhythmic gait. She was accustomed to movement for women, and Ted found it embarrassing to move to such poetic Bliss Carman measures as "The wind went combing through the grass; the lithe young daisies swayed and bowed."

There was much that was foolish, silly, even a little sad about Mrs. King's training, but there was a great deal that Ted was able to sift out that proved useful to him and at least prepared him to a degree for the invaluable lessons he was to have some years later with Mrs. Hovey herself. Mrs. King, however, thought she had something going for her in Norma and Ted and wrote a vaudeville skit about an Irish maid and an Irish policeman meeting in a New York park and discovering they had both come from the same part of the old sod. Ted protested that he hadn't come east and paid a lot of money just for a vaudeville act, but Mrs. King was at a loss to know what else to do for him. He was too old for ballet and too big for the swaying daisy school of movement, so she told him bluntly that he'd better forget dancing—he'd never make it. In the years ahead he delighted in sending Mrs. King ecstatic reviews from all over the United States and, indeed, the world.

Back in New York he and Norma obtained some dancing dates.

Enough people asked the handsome young man if he taught his own highly original way of dance to others so that he rented a studio by the hour and began making money as a teacher. More and more pupils enrolled. One day a girl, Marielle Moller, came to him and said she had a chance for a job if, in a matter of days, she could come up with four new dances with new costumes and musical arrangements. Ted refused but she talked him into it. She wasn't, he remembered, a very good dancer, but he made her some numbers that he described as "foolproof," and she got the job and made a hit. Naturally, she became a devoted pupil.

One day, out of the blue, Marielle casually dropped the news that she had been a guest of Ruth St. Denis at a party. Ted was bowled over. Could she get him an invitation? He wanted to study Oriental dance with his idol. Did she ever teach? Marielle carried back the word to Brother St. Denis. Brother, as well as Mother, were the dragons protecting their genius. Brother came to see Ted dance at a benefit and decided he was manly, personable, and talented and that his sister should see him. Ruth St. Denis's memories of this period were a little different. She recalled that her managers insisted she include some exhibition ballroom dances on her program and that the public would require such additions. She was not interested but agreed that one of the girls in her company might do such dances with a partner. She sent out a call for male dancers. Brother auditioned them. He selected Ted. Whichever story is true, a meeting was arranged, and Ted Shawn went to the great star's studio to meet her for tea.

As he waited for her, he admired and thrilled to the photographs and posters of this exotic, black-haired, dark-skinned goddess. He was lost in his fantasies when he heard a clomp and clatter of shoes coming down a staircase. "Not even a maid should be permitted to make such a racket in this temple, in this home of a goddess," he thought. And then the clomper appeared, pale-skinned, white-haired, sloppily dressed, ordinary. She held out her hand. Ruth St. Denis had entered his life. For good and for evil, for triumph and abasement, for ecstasy and unbearable torture, she stayed there until death released him at eighty.

5

Ruth St. Denis and Ted Shawn talked. They talked until dinner time. St. Denis invited Shawn to remain for dinner. He needed no coaxing but simply mentioned that at eight thirty he had to give a private dance lesson to a Polish countess. Eight thirty came and went and midnight arrived. An appointment was made for the next day and the talk resumed. It continued, with certain spectacular interruptions, for over fifty years.

No one knows who dominated the conversation at that first meeting. Both were talkers. Presumably young Ted poured forth his admiration for the great star in floods of poetry mixed with metaphysical comments about the art of dancing. And surely St. Denis held forth on her philosophies, "pontificating," at length, as she later described her occasional bits of sermonizing to pupils, friends, the press.

My personal guess is that the first conversation and all those which followed during their stormy marriage and mellow reunions in later years were all contests. Dancers associated with the St. Denis-Shawn companies over the years recall that if they weren't talking to each other, they were reading out loud to their students and casts in studios, trains, hotel lobbies, making comments on what they had just read.

I remember them together on many occasions. The air was always electrically charged. It was exciting to be near them, but one always felt that in that electrified atmosphere a short circuit could easily occur. Long after they had separated and made some sort of a peace, she would visit his summertime dance festival, often to perform or teach for him, and at lunch or dinner, the conversation would be resumed. People at the table remained silent—they were expected to do so—and Ted would sit at the head of the table, presiding, with Ruth at his right. She ate heartily. He barely touched his food as he held forth on St. Denis-Shawn reminiscences or on some one of his accomplishments. She, with perfect timing, would delicately chew her underlip (a St. Denis trademark of polite attention indicative of a pounce on the prey to come) and wait for him to catch his breath. At that instant she would leap into the contest and take over with a totally different view of the same anecdote, this time making herself the center of the story. Masterfully she would proceed until she had eliminated all mention of him.

It was reciprocal, however. When she arrived at Jacob's Pillow, the site of Shawn's festival, for their fiftieth anniversary celebration, she was met by her husband, closeted with him for some time, and then permitted to walk to her cottage. En route, she ran into Shawn's composer-pianist, Jess Meeker, who said, "Hi! Miss Ruth. How are you? How was the trip from Hollywood?" To which she replied, "Thank you for asking about me, Jess. All I've heard for the last three hours is Ted Shawn, Ted Shawn, Ted Shawn!"

The talk contest started in 1914.

When Ruth St. Denis entered Ted Shawn's life as a partner, someone else had to make an exit. The exiter was Norma Gould. She wasn't at all happy about it, for although Ted had added artistic stimulation and financial rewards to her life in Los Angeles, he had drawn her out of her own independent orbit and made her career a part, subsidiary in retrospect, of his own career. It was he who wanted to travel to New York and he needed a partner, a female dancer, for the essential Sante Fe bookings.

Once engaged by St. Denis, Ted had no further need for Norma. He did not, of course, simply eliminate her from his life. But he justified the break, as he did his parting earlier with Hazel and as he would do in other associations for the rest of his life, in a way that placed the decision, if not the actual blame, on the offended party.

He recalled that when he learned that Brother St. Denis had approved a contract, he expected that Addie Munn (Adelaide Montgomery of the Santa Fe tour) and Norma Gould would be delighted. That Norma would be "delighted" to lose her partner seemed logical to him because he felt she would be cheering his good fortune, and if she had romantic feelings for him, he was unaware of it. His justification was further expressed years later when he wrote: "There had never been any contract, written or verbal, between Norma and me. We had drifted into our partnership in California, and jointly took the Santa Fe tour because both of us wanted to come east and study. It was more or less understood" (by whom, we might wish to ask!) "that Norma definitely planned to return to California to go on teaching, and I thought equally understood that I did not want to or intend to return to California if I could do anything else. However, Norma was deeply hurt at what she interpreted as my breaking up of our partnership. After much argument, during which she stuck to her point of view, I returned to 89th Street and told Brother and Ruth that much as it grieved me to do so, I would have to refuse the engagement, for although I had not considered myself contracted to go with Norma, since she felt that way, I felt honor bound to go on with her."

St. Denis and Brother, eager to have Ted, agreed to take Norma into the company to dance with Ted those ballroom dances which the managers felt essential to the repertory. Ted was commissioned by the St. Denises to offer the job to Norma—they did not interview her themselves nor even audition her—and, as he reported, "Norma, realizing that this offer was made for the single purpose of getting me into the company, didn't show any great joy." She accepted grudgingly.

Rehearsals began, but a week before leaving for the opening of the tour in Paducah, Kentucky, "inner conflict having achieved its disruptive end," wrote Ted, "Norma had a complete nervous breakdown and it was decided that Addie would take her back to California, and Norma released me to go on with Ruth St. Denis." The hysterics took place on a Thursday. On Monday Ruth St. Denis, with Ted Shawn, opened happily in Paducah. Alice Martin, who had been engaged to perform exhibition ballroom dances with Brother on the St. Denis program, had been replaced by Norma and Ted, and now Norma was gone. Ted noted a very pretty girl in the company and felt that with some fast coaching she would be ideal for him. Her name was Hilda Beyer, and although she was not a trained dancer and had been used by St. Denis chiefly as a decorative "super" in the Oriental dances, Ted instructed her in the tango, maxixe, hesitation waltz, and other social dances on the train traveling to Paducah. Shawn and Beyer became a successful team in the St. Denis group until St. Denis herself decided that she would have a whirl at popular dance.

In Paducah Ted Shawn and Ruth St. Denis appeared on stage together for the first time. And for the first time, with countless such times to follow, he was angry with her on matters of billing. It read:

RUTH ST. DENIS
assisted by
Hilda Beyer and Ted Shawn

For the moment—but not for long—he acquiesced in top billing for St. Denis, but as for the rest he noted that it was "not in accord with the promises made to me. I was, even though compared with Ruth, not well known, an established dancer, having had my own school in Los Angeles, and having done a moving picture, and a tour from California to New York—and Hilda, as we all well knew, was not yet even a dancer, much less a name."

His ego was further affronted by the first review which said, "Miss Hilda Beyer danced divinely the Blue Danube and various modern ballroom dances. She was ably supported by Mr. Ted Shawn." Ted decided that the critic must be a male and that he must have been "bemused by Hilda's physical charms." Nonetheless, when the new ballroom duo proved popular during performances at Chicago's Ravinia Park, he was delighted to be held over with Hilda, while St. Denis moved on to other commitments.

But his initial tour provided the groundwork for an historic partnership. Ruth and Ted not only danced but in Paducah, Topeka, and a host of other cities east of the Mississippi, they continued that intense conversation which had started at their first meeting. The topics were esthetic, philosophical, theosophical, visionary; they were also romantic. Both were dedicated to God and Art. St. Denis, she was soon to discover, was also dedicated to Love, an area she had suppressed for all of her thirty-six years, partly out of fear of sex and partly because she was watched over and protected by Mother St. Denis. In her old age, nearing ninety, she would say to me, "I have worshipped three Gods: the God of Art, the God of Physical

Love, the God in Heaven. And I have been unfaithful to all three."
With Ted she was about to discover the God of Physical Love.

For some reason, long since forgotten, Mother St. Denis did not
go on this fateful tour. Perhaps she felt that Ruthie would be well
guarded by Brother. Such was not the case.

Ruth was lonesome. Ted was someone to talk to and with. He
worshipped her. He behaved like an acolyte. He was handsome. Soon
he was able to combine his awe of her with ardor. He told her about
his romance with Hazel, and he showed her the poetry—or "bad
verse" as he later called it—which he had written when they had
broken off the engagement. Ruth wept for the bereft young man.
This drew them closer, for St. Denis, despite her inexorable drive
for her own continuing preeminence, was a sentimentalist. In Norfolk, Virginia, the twenty-two-year-old student-disciple proposed
marriage to his thirty-six-year-old (or perhaps she was really older)
teacher-goddess.

The arguments began. Ruth didn't want to marry. She indicated
that an affair, since Mother wasn't around, might be a solution. Ted
would have none of it. "Sexually, my standards were simple and un-
complicated. You kept yourself 'pure' for the woman you would one
day marry. When you found her, you married her, and then had
your physical experiences." He, presumably still a virgin, was adamant for marriage; she was adamant against it.

His stand, looking at it from today, would seem to be not as
simple as he made it. Certainly, with his ministerial background, his
genuine involvement with religion, his moral stance would be expected. But was there something more in his holding aloof from an
affair? Here was the most famous woman he had ever met and, in
his new world of dance, the most important one. How long would
an illicit romance last? Could its termination end a professional partnership? Marriage was not so easily dissolved. No one can ever be
certain that there was calculation there. Ted Shawn, in his relationships with women who had been useful to his career, had been
shrewd. Now he could embark on a relationship beyond which, in
dance, there would be no further need for advancement. I wonder if
he thought of this or sensed it.

St. Denis didn't want to be trapped. She didn't want to be

trapped on May 4, 1914, in Norfolk and she didn't want to be trapped in the years ahead. In fact she kept trying to escape Ted Shawn off and on throughout their joint career of nearly twenty years. She left him many times and returned—to be fair to him in such matters of marital accord—when it suited her to do so or when she needed him to support her career.

Her basic antipathy to marriage was centered in her own spirit of independence. She had been an independent performer since 1896, and she had been an international star since 1906. She had become accustomed to her own superior position. Not only did she refuse young Ted equal billing, she was not about to take offstage billing as Mrs. Shawn. This feeling about marriage was compounded by two factors: her genuine fear of motherhood and her subjugation by her own mother.

Her best friend in her days as a Belasco actress-dancer was Honoria Donner, her beloved "Patsy," a pretty girl and the one who listened to Ruthie's wild dreams of a dance that didn't exist and helped her bring those impossible dreams to reality in the rough two years when Ruth was making the transition from show business to art. Patsy got married when her Belasco engagements were over. Ruth, after her American debut as an innovator, traveled to Europe for three years of triumphs. When she returned, she discovered that her dearest friend had had a baby a year, had lost her good looks, and lived what seemed to Ruth a squalid life with an unprepossessing husband. To Ruth, who dramatized everything, the awful image of Patsy's life was the awful definition of marriage. She wanted none of it.

Mother had also kept her daughter virginal. Her own marriage was not a smashing success, for Father was given to drink and although he was a gifted man and an inventor of more than fleeting accomplishments, he was utterly improvident. Mother was a brilliant woman but a breakdown had turned her away from medicine, and she had found strength in a philosophy which ultimately led her and her daughter into Christian Science. In Ruth's career, the mother found her own fulfillment, and because her daughter's creative genius was guided by very little in the way of discipline, she herself provided the disciplines, both theatrical and personal.

When Ruth was a teen-age show girl, Mother permitted the great architect and celebrated ladies' man, Stanford White, to see her daughter, but she chaperoned all outings and she permitted no lavish gifts such as White gave to other actresses. Mother allowed Mr. White to give Ruthie a bicycle which she used to get from home in Brooklyn to Manhattan and back. Later she presided over an intense but Platonic romance between Ruth and the famed European critic and poet, Hugo von Hofmannsthal, librettist for the Richard Strauss opera *Electra*. Mother was certainly not going to lose her daughter to an ambitious twenty-two-year-old youth who had been hired to do some ballroom dances, at the manager's request, in her daughter's company.

When Ruth returned to Mother in July while Ted and Hilda were playing the outdoor theater at Chicago's Ravinia (Ted got his top billing then—he saw to that), there were not only arguments but hysterics. Ruth, who didn't want to marry, now got stubborn when Mother forbade her to take the step. Ted returned to a household of daily sobbing, for he had rented a room in the same building where the St. Denises lived. And it was his turn to take on the terrifying matriarch.

Ted described her "Protean tactics" as including "storms of rage, ridicule, pathetic helplessness, and calm appeals to common sense." Ted was adamant. He and Ruth could, of course, get married, but she was still so close to her mother's domination that she would not make a move without her. Ted, on his part, wanted the old lady's consent. He wanted it stated clearly and irrevocably. He wore down Mother St. Denis, who finally admitted defeat and called her thirty-six-year-old child to her and said, "Ruthie, I respect that young man—I do not think marriage is wise for you, but if you must, marry him. But I *warn* you, he's no weakling!" With that prediction, Mother retired into the background. She lived for many more years but the tie with her daughter gradually became merely sentimental.

With Mother's approval won, Ruth began to vacillate. Ted felt that she had fully expected her mother to say no to the proposal, thereby relieving Ruthie of a decision. Now it was back with her. She summoned up all of Mother's reasons for having originally disapproved of the match, reiterated her own, combined them. But Ted was not about to embark on any relationship which did not seem to promise permanence. He continued his suit. Early in the morning of

August 13, 1914, Ruth St. Denis went to Ted Shawn and said, "Come on, let's go down to City Hall and get this thing over with."

Ruth was wearing an inexpensive, unpressed blue serge suit and a cheap blue straw hat. (St. Denis once said to me, in the 1960s, that she could look back and remember that she had taken a sort of perverse pride in being the worst-dressed star in the American theater.) At the license bureau she stood in line behind Mamie O'Leary and, as Ruth Dennis, differed from Mamie only in that Mamie had been married three times before and was vague about the names of the first trio as she prepared to take on a fourth.

The license in hand, they went to a one-time Congregational minister who had turned to Christian Science but had retained his right to perform marriages. The St. Denis family insisted that the marriage be kept secret since in that era married stars were not considered glamorous, and more than one movie celebrity lost both fans and contracts when secret marriages came to light. Ruth insisted that the word "obey" be omitted from the ceremony, she refused to wear a wedding ring, since it was a sign of bondage, and she shuddered at the legal term, "married woman," a designation she abhorred with all the contempt of a forerunner of women's liberation.

The service was composed of several Protestant selections, combined with suitable remarks from Mary Baker Eddy's *Science and Health*. Brother St. Denis and his wife, Emily, were the witnesses. Brother and Emily had caused Mother great anguish before Ruth and Ted repeated the affront. Emily had been Emily Purkis, a wardrobe mistress in the theater. She had worked in a theater across the street from where Ruth St. Denis had performed in David Belasco's *Zaza* in London in 1899, but she did not meet Brother until later in America, where she had come to work in wardrobe. Mother St. Denis was violently against the match. Shawn told me in later years that Mother at one time had referred to Emily as a chambermaid. But Brother was not dominated by his mother, although he was devoted to his sister. Even Ruth did not approve his marriage, and for the next half century, when she was in a particularly bitchy mood, would indicate that she felt "Buzz" had married below his station. Brother and Emily had a continuously happy married life, and Emily and Ruth died the same year, 1968, in houses, both built and owned by Brother, separated by only a patio.

Ted also had a conflict of wills with Brother. There was nothing overt, but Ted, consciously or subconsciously, was quickly removing the influences of the past from his new wife and consolidating his own position in her life. I saw Ted and Brother together—in amiable confrontation—only once. It was in 1969 at Jacob's Pillow, and Brother had flown east from his Hollywood home to attend a program which I had arranged, at Ted's request, in memory of Miss Ruth. It was based on a Buddhist idea, which Ted wanted, to skip a memorial service right after a funeral in order to permit mourning to pass and, a year later, to "celebrate." We did that for Ruth St. Denis. Brother was well past eighty at the time, Ted nearly eighty. The two old men looked each other over and Buzz, who had a rather racy approach toward life, said, "Well, Ted, your legs are in better shape than mine"—Buzz was using a cane—"but from the legs up, I'm better off than you are!" and he gave a broad smile and a wink to the ladies present in the room.

But in 1914 Brother was shortly to leave his post as Ruth's lighting genius, stage manager, companion, and protector. Mother was already receding into the background. Ruth needed watching and guiding and discipline. The Prussian descendant of the von Schauns was ready for the job.

The job, and the pleasure, of husband he was not permitted to fulfill at first. Stubbornly Ruth reasserted her antagonism to the subservient role of the wife, to the "bondage" of marriage, to the mastery of the male. She did not permit the marriage to be fully consummated until some time in October, two months after the start of a nine-month tour of one-night stands.

He wanted desperately to become a father, but she not only had no interest in children, she wished no interruption of her career and, with the picture of Patsy Donner engraved in her mind, she was certain that childbirth would destroy the beauty of her body, a body which had brought gasps of appreciation from the public and the paeans of poets and artists, including even the great sculptor Rodin. But once she had satisfied herself that her contraceptive methods were safe, she gave herself wholeheartedly to the sexual experience. The release strengthened their marriage ties and, indeed, served to keep them together even when professional differences, ambitions, and jealousies tended to tear them apart. The release spilled over the marriage confines as far as St. Denis was concerned, and throughout much of their time together she was often unfaithful to him. He did not disapprove of this morally but I believe it affronted his vanity to such an extent that eventually he had to prove his own desirability to others.

The honeymoon tour opened in Saratoga, New York, on August 19, 1914, and terminated in San Francisco on March 2, 1915. Kansas City, where Ted had been born, was on the route. He had hoped for a hero's homecoming, but he found instead the typical provincial reaction to the boy who leaves home, "What does Teddy think he is, decked out in all those clothes!" But it was here, during an interview, that Ruth herself, charmed by a woman reporter, took her into her confidence and told her, off the record she thought, that she and Ted were married. The next day in the *Kansas City Star* and on several front pages across the nation appeared pictures of the two along with the headline, RUTH ST. DENIS MARRIES TED SHAWN—THE MOST BEAUTIFUL MAN IN THE WORLD.

The unlikely description of Shawn, who was handsome but hardly beautiful, was born of a confusion of identities. Big in vaudeville in those days was Paul Swan, a painter who had decided to become a dancer because of his beauty of face and body. Swan never had a dance lesson, fearing it would mar his natural grace. He had been taken up by New York society, built a repertory of mime-dances—Pavlova's *The Dying Swan* and, of course, something called "Narcissus" among them. There were feature stories in Sunday newspaper supplements about this man who was quite willing to be billed The Most Beautiful Man in the World.

Ted had seen him at a performance soon after he and Norma had come to New York and had found him truly beautiful to look at when he was motionless but appalling when he began to dance. Ted noted that Swan's features were as perfect as those to be found on a Greek coin and that his body was faultlessly proportioned. But he cringed at chiffon bows worn at the neck and wrist and rouge used on the buttocks as well as on the upper cheeks. Performers such as Swan, he felt, undid all that he himself was attempting to do in erasing the long-held view that dancing was an effeminate activity for men.

Shawn complained vigorously about the misnomer, and the matter was corrected in the press but the harm had been done and "the stigma," which he felt it to be, was attached to him for several years.

The tour itself proved to be a complete justification of Shawn's value to Ruth St. Denis. She had been triumphant from 1906 to 1910, but then poor management, bad judgment, and ridiculous production expenses on her part, inferior publicity, and faulty planning had nearly ruined her career. Ted Shawn changed all that. A European tour had been planned originally so that St. Denis could return to the scenes of her 1906 to 1909 German successes. But the war ended these major projects abruptly. With pressures from Shawn the last-minute coast-to-coast tour materialized, growing from some sporadic bookings to a tightly packed money-making period. St. Denis would be out of debt at last, and the future seemed bright.

In San Francisco Ruth St. Denis and Ted Shawn presented their first joint choreographic effort, *The Garden of Kama*. The theme was an East Indian story of a girl of quality who withdrew from the advances of the god of love but was wooed in the moonlight by a handsome young fisherman. The fisherman was, of course, Kama in disguise, the god who never failed. It was an immediate success, and although Shawn, in his early writings (*Ruth St. Denis: Pioneer and Prophet*), credits the choreography to St. Denis, later comments indicate that he was an important factor in its creation.

Indeed, it was in the capacity of editor and taskmaster that Shawn took over from Mother St. Denis. Ruth was overflowing with creative ideas, and it was essential for someone to stem the tide from time to time. She would compose a dance in a studio and either forget what she had done the day before or weary of it and invent something new. She was a genius at dance improvisation, and going on stage without a definite routine did not bother her one whit. Ted used to say in the 1960s that even in those dances dating back to 1906 and performed for half a century, "Ruth really had only a general choreographic outline and a few key poses at the end of key phrases in mind when she went on stage. The in-betweens were pure instinct."

Long before there was a Ted, Mother would pamper her daughter for a few days, then, at a rehearsal, would stand up and say, "Ruthie, whatever you have just done, stays. No more changes."

And Ruth would scream and rage that she had to experiment more to find what she really wanted. Mother would be adamant, and a dance would become as set as possible. This discipline was essential in dances involving more than St. Denis herself. She could improvise, but she could not expect a company to find its way around the stage in the midst of her spur-of-the-moment dance excursions. With Mother out of the staging end Ted was the disciplinarian. It was an almost hopeless job.

It was on the tour which saw the creation of *The Garden of Kama* that the name that was later used to describe an American dance epoch was coined. In the repertory was a number called the *Ruth St. Denis Mazurka,* which had been designed to answer the public's interest in social dances and, perhaps, to serve as a nonballet counterpart to Pavlova's enormously popular *Gavotte.* The manager of the Heilig Theater in Portland, Oregon, felt he needed a gimmick to bolster ticket sales, so he convinced St. Denis and Shawn that they should pretend that the *Mazurka* was a brand-new number made for Portland especially and that he would offer a prize (free seats) to the best title for the dance. The winning name was *The Denishawn Rose Mazurka,* the "rose" for Portland, which was known as "The Rose City." No one ever met the woman who won, and no one ever found out whether she used her free tickets, but the name was destined to stick. This was February 1915.

In the summer of 1915 Ruth St. Denis and Ted Shawn looked back on a tour that had paid back ten thousand dollars of the St. Denis debts piled up from pre-Shawn enterprises; a raise in salary, from forty dollars a week to sixty dollars a week for Shawn himself; and what appeared to be a successful partnership. They were in California. Ted had had a booming dance school business in Los Angeles. Why not start again? The two decided to open a new kind of school, however, an academy of dance and its related arts with classes in as many dance techniques as they could offer, music, drama, stage, and costume design. They found a house set high above the street and with spacious lawns and a pool; they built a huge outdoor studio, tented, to augment the rooms that could be used for classes. Students' fees were dropped into a cigar box at the studio door. Mother and Father Dennis and Brother's Emily were instructed to give up the house in New York and move west.

Opening day arrived and students saw for the first time the name of an entirely new school, style, concept of American dance: Denishawn. The name was to appear on studio doors, properly franchised, throughout the United States and on playbills and posters and in headlines around the world. Denishawn had been born. Perhaps its death was also presaged in the school's subtitle, which the senior director had insisted upon: The Ruth St. Denis School of the Dance and Its Related Arts.

There was no mention of Ted Shawn.

6

With the founding of Denishawn, Ted Shawn stated the artistic creed which was to guide the school, the company and, indeed, his whole life in dance. It was his own wording of a concept which he and St. Denis had arrived at after weeks of discussion and planning. It went: "The art of the dance is too big to be encompassed by any one system. On the contrary the dance includes all systems or schools of dance. Every way that any human being of any race or nationality, at any period of human history, has moved rhythmically to express himself, belongs to the dance. We endeavor to recognize and use all contributions of the past to the dance and will continue to include all new contributions in the future."

This was a revolutionary esthetic concept at the time, yet years later, when some of the most distinguished products of that system (or lack of system) left Denishawn and rebelled against its principles, the main reason for the defection was that this concept was too eclectic to produce anything worthwhile. Yet it had, unarguably, produced Martha Graham, Doris Humphrey, and Charles Weidman, the chief founders in the 1920s of America's modern dance.

The school attracted students of all kinds. There were the girls whose mothers wanted them to learn to be graceful, a standard aspect of any dancing school. There were those who dreamed of careers as dancers, perhaps in the Denishawn Company itself! And there were movie stars, for indeed the greats of Hollywood flocked to the new school in order to extend their own performing knowledge, to learn dance routines that might well be needed in the elaborate movies of the day, and, of course, to acquire new mimetic skills so essential to the silent screen. Among the first was Lillian Gish, who was to appear with Roszika Dolly (one half of the then famous

67

Dolly Sisters) in a movie called *The Lily and the Rose*—the fragile, virginal Gish was, of course, the Lily. Ted created a dance, cool and gentle, for Gish, and St. Denis choreographed a sensual East Indian dance for Rosy Dolly, who was to play the Rose. Both continued their dance studies long after their routines were set and filmed.

There were other stars of the day, most of them coming from the Broadway stage to become a part of the new and lucrative movie industry, who turned to Denishawn for assistance. Very often they would ask Ted or, if an Oriental style were needed, St. Denis to stage for them or coach them in a dance required by a movie script. Louise Glaum, a big vamp figure of the day, needed sinuous routines. An intensely dramatic actress such as Ruth Chatterton or a polished comedienne of the Ina Claire order might be required by a script to perform a new social dance or a segment of a dance in historical period style and costumes. Where else to go but to the most talked about new dance school in Los Angeles, Denishawn? Like Dolly and Gish, several of the stars, even after the assigned routines were learned and filmed, would return to Denishawn for lessons in dance. Chatterton for one, who remained a major figure throughout a long career which made her a superstar in the early talking films and always a popular legitimate performer, remained a close friend of Ted Shawn's, always insisting that dance training was essential to the actor.

Both the principal Denishawners choreographed not only star-focused dances for movies but also vast dance spectacles, enormously popular in the great days of silent films when spectacle was a special Hollywood product.

It was Ruth who choreographed the vast Babylonian ballets for D. W. Griffith's historic *Intolerance*, although she herself, contrary to general belief and subsequent credits in movie museums, did not perform in it. She told me once, "I did the dances for *Intolerance* but I never set foot before the cameras. Some dame in a couple of breastplates was mistaken for me, and I've been haunted by her ever since in the wrong captions for display posters, in books, everywhere."

The Denishawns, according to Agnes de Mille, also attracted a wholly new kind of student, girls from good families. De Mille, who lived in Hollywood at the time because both her father, William, and her uncle, Cecil, were important men of the movies, recently said to me, "Parents could send their children to Denishawn because Ruth and Ted were something very rare, they were respectable. They were respectable because they were married."

Except for private lessons and the teaching of routines the Denishawn pupil paid one dollar for lessons from Ruth St. Denis and Ted Shawn, plus a lunch which was composed of stew or a rice dish and bread and fruit. Shawn started them off with general exercising—stretching, limbering, breathing—and then went on to a beginning ballet level, including the fundamental training steps at the ballet *barre*. St. Denis would teach Oriental or, at any rate, her concept of Oriental dancing (mainly East Indian), most of which she had invented herself. (This was ten years before she went to India to captivate that public with the same kind of nonauthentic but spiritually profound, brilliantly theatrical extensions of ancient Indian dances.) In addition she taught movement forms derived from her dances (most of her academic approach reversed the customary method of employing a technique for preparation of a dance and, instead, extracted technique materials from a theater piece). She worked with her students in experiments in moving in silence yet in rhythmic forms, and in contrast, with complex orchestral structure.

Shawn was also experimenting with new movement idioms, with what might be described as "free-style" (or no-period style) movement exercises planned simply to develop the muscle skills of the body. He also began to explore, at first in a very elementary way but later in great depth, the meaningful-movement principles of the nineteenth-century French scientist of psychologically revelatory movement, François Delsarte.

A case may be made that America's modern dance is rooted in Delsarte principles and that Ted Shawn, who became the world's foremost dance authority on Delsarte, nurtured those roots. Back in 1915, however, his exposure to Delsarte had been limited to his lessons with Mary Perry King—it was not until later that he realized that Mrs. King's methods had been uncredited, bastardized versions of Delsartean gestural expressions—and to the fact that St. Denis, through her mother (who had been a pupil of a pupil of Delsarte's), had been applying, without realizing it, some Delsarte principles to her own dances. But who, or what, was Delsarte?

He had been a French operatic tenor who had lost his voice

through bad training. He stopped singing and began looking at opera. He found the acting ridiculous. So as he began to coach young singers, he became more and more concerned with movements of the body. He never danced. He never taught a dancer. His investigations of human behavior came at a time when dance was about to shed its surface garments of decorative movement and probe the meanings of movement.

Over the years Delsarte studied the gestures, the movement behavior of mothers, of nursemaids, of lovers, of prisoners, of the dying, the exulting. He recorded his discoveries, analyzed them and classified them. The body was divided into zones (upper, middle, lower), and the limbs were similarly divided; the space in which they moved (up, out, down) was similarly defined. To these zones he applied such qualities as spiritual, intellectual (head-neck, upper air, hands, feet); emotional (shoulders, chest and torso, lower arms, middle space); physical, in strength or sexuality (hips, pelvis and thighs, space close to earth).

The Delsarte system was complex. In the 1880s and 1890s it had been misinterpreted and misused by elocutionists who wanted to underscore words with gesture, by ham actors. Delsarte rules, watered down and distorted, became the rage in Europe and America. There were Delsarte clothes, Delsarte shoes (like Mary Perry King's shoes on rockers for a rolling, rhythmic gait), Delsarte corsets to control bodily beauty, and even Delsarte wooden legs! This was the bastardization. Steele McKaye, a major American actor and a pupil of Delsarte, stood for the correct principles and abjured the stock gestures others had evolved. Genevieve Stebbins, an early expressional dancer, had influenced St. Denis, through a concert of expressive movement, in the 1880s; and Mrs. Richard Hovey, a pupil of Delsarte, heard of the new Denishawn, saw Ted, admired him, offered to help, and instituted what are believed to have been the first Delsarte classes applied to the needs of the dancer . . . at Denishawn.

To free-style movements, to adapted ballet, to derived Orientalisms, to Delsarte, Ted added experiments with male movements, mostly in terms of physical strength. Women, for example, tended to make gestures which came from wrists or elbow, occasionally, the shoulder. Men, working in fields and forests or wielding weapons, accomplished arm movements from the strength of the back, from the powerful *latissimus dorsi* muscles so highly developed (or potentially so) in the male. Everything Ted Shawn could think of, every kind of movement experience which came into his ken was grist for Denishawn.

This concept of dance education, launched at the first Denishawn in 1915, would constitute Ted Shawn's educational creed for the rest of his long life. He watched it grow from a Los Angeles base to national acceptance; he saw it culminate, in terms of the establishment, in the building of Denishawn House in New York City in 1927, the first building in America to be designed specifically for dance; later he saw it rejected by the rebellious young moderns who launched the modern dance movement just as Greater Denishawn was in the making; and he lived to see his creed reaffirmed in the 1950s, 1960s and 1970s as dance schools and universities expanded programs to include ballet, modern dance, all forms of ethnic dance, jazz, mime, and more, just as Denishawn had envisioned a half century before but in less sophisticated, less knowledgeable form.

The theatrical approach, of course, paralleled the training methods. A spectacular example of what Denishawn stood for theatrically, in terms of theme, choreography, and lavish production, is well illustrated by *A Dance Pageant of Egypt, Greece, and India*, produced in 1916 at the huge open-air Greek Theater at the University of California at Berkeley. The Denishawns were the first dancers to be permitted by the board of trustees to perform in the ten-thousand-seat theater, presumably because they were "respectable" and because their themes seemed, geographically at least, educational. The cast included forty dancers from the Denishawn Company and school, one hundred or more students from the university, the university chorus, and the San Francisco Symphony Orchestra.

Ruth St. Denis was the star. Ted Shawn was the featured supporting artist. The small professional Denishawn Company was highlighted. Among the student dancers was a newcomer, a college graduate only two years younger than Ted Shawn; her name was Martha Graham.

There were three acts to the pageant, and each act was divided into two sections, for the plan of the work was to show the life as lived of each nation and also its beliefs in an afterlife. The whole section on Egypt contained scenes originally created by St. Denis for her historic *Egypta* (1910), but there were new passages of considerable innovative force. The Denishawn penchant for striking production was evident at the opening when the cast of 170, with each dancer covered by individual trailing veils of green and white (each dyed by Ted himself), swirled onto the stage in imitation of the inundation of the Nile (St. Denis had suggested this in her *Egypta*). As the river receded, dancers emerged to indicate the presence of man. The first two, born of the fecundity of the Nile, were St. Denis and Shawn, the female and the male who plowed and sowed and reaped, fished and hunted, and drew a living from the land. This duet, called "Tillers of the Soil," was very probably the first dance ever created on the theme of the labors of men. (Years later, of course, Ted would do his all-male *Labor Symphony* of men's work in the fields, on the seas, in the forest, and in the factories.) "Tillers" was so successful that it remained as a duet in the Denishawn repertory.

In the section on Greece Ted composed his first all-male group dance, a Pyrrhic dance for sixteen young men, which was also very probably the first dance created for men only in the history of the Western theater. It was performed alone in the huge space and received the loudest and longest applause of any number, including St. Denis-Shawn duets, in the pageant.

The director of the Greek Theater was Professor William Armes. It was he who had convinced the board of trustees that if Greek drama had been acceptable to the theater then certainly dance, which the ancient Greeks revered, should have a place in that theater. It was also his duty to see that the conservative members of the board and the conventional members of the audience not be offended in any way. St. Denis had long glorified the beauty of the body and had been criticized across the country not simply because some of her dances called for a bare midriff but also because she performed in bare feet! Ted too was given to exposure. Professor Armes realized that fleshings (as body tights were then called) were used by the dancers but he pleaded rather pitifully that they be made to look more like coverings than simulated nudity.

The professor got more (or, rather, less!) than he reckoned for in the India section. St. Denis, as the wife of a slain hero, was to commit suttee, that is, to throw herself on her husband's funeral pyre and die upon his death. At dress rehearsal, because the stars had been so busy checking the costumes of the vast troupe, St. Denis forgot to put on the total Hindu dress. She heard her cue, rushed on, and, ripping off her long sari, threw herself on her husband's inert body. To her consternation and his, she discovered that she had not remembered the *choli*, the little jacket worn under the sari. It was too late to do anything about it, so bare-bosomed, she cast herself onto the dead prince, murmuring as she collapsed, "Oh, dear, dear, Professor Armes is never going to stand for this!"

In fact the pageant was an enormous success. It was later redesigned for indoor showing in Los Angeles and outdoors at San Diego, redesigned and reduced yet again for inclusion on the long (forty unbroken weeks averaging fourteen performances a week) vaudeville and concert tour which was to follow. The pageant material had also contained dances which St. Denis had performed before, not only the *Egypta* excerpts but also her famed *The Incense*, which had first captivated Ted in Denver, some Nautch dances, and other East Indian numbers which a predance Shawn had marveled at in 1911.

The touring repertory also offered a staged version of a Denishawn class, thus publicizing the new concept of dance training from basic exercises through ballet to Oriental forms and music interpretation numbers, as well as non-Oriental dances based on nature studies and musical forms and St. Denis's ever popular solo, *The Peacock*, in which she played a beautiful woman so enamored of her own charms that she was transformed into a peacock in punishment for her vanity.

St. Denis hated the drudgery of the tour. She felt fettered by the unending demands of travel and performance; her soul she thought was being crushed and her creative desires smothered. It was true that she had, of course, been performing steadily for twenty years by this time and she had done her stint in vaudeville, starting with her eleven shows a day back in 1896. She wanted to get out, but the bookings paid the bills and gave her money for the ever more elaborate productions she had in mind. Ted adored it. He was so much younger and he had really just commenced his career. He was as eager to dance in Kanakee as in New York and he learned to go on, as troupers always do, with bleeding feet, broken toes, a dislocated back, flu, dysentery—every disease which besets travelers plus those to which dancers are subject.

Ruth tended to let down and Mother, growing old in Hollywood, wasn't there to keep her daughter in tow. Ted tried, but he was reminded that although he was husband and lover, equality ended right there. While he had bested other influences, St. Denis was boss. There were bitter battles between the two, and only the still fresh force of their love affair postponed a rift that was destined to come between the self-centered, disorganized, mercurial genius and the younger, talented, highly businesslike and ambitious husband.

In the summer of 1917 the Denishawn School moved to a larger building as the enrollment swelled, and an assisting faculty made it possible to add further classes to the curriculum.

It was a significant year in other ways. The combination of St. Denis and Shawn, through the long transcontinental tour, had made an impact on the public both with respect to the comparatively sophisticated (though understandably ignorant in dance matters) concert-going audience eager for new esthetic experiences and the vaudeville public which wanted a good show. Denishawn served both. This dual appeal is of major importance in assessing the place of Denishawn in the American theater. Exotic themes, gorgeous costumes, increasingly lavish sets, romantic themes attracted a public that would have avoided a sparer form of dance or would have been bored with the loping and skipping of the school-recital type of "fancy dancing." In a word, the Denishawners brought serious dance art to the public but made it palatable through skillful production methods. A decade later, when the modern dance came into being, Denishawn would be dismissed as superficial, as "show biz," and the criticism was leveled at Shawn far more than at St. Denis.

When *Time* Magazine was butchering Ted in the 1930s with the use of dreadful photos from his earliest days and cruelly isolated quotes, I assumed that someone had a personal vendetta going with him. Why else would they use a picture of him, taken twenty years before and showing him with too much makeup (acceptable in the early movie days) and a spit curl, and pair it with a straight report about his taking an all-male troupe to London for a major engagement? When he got furious at a noisy audience in the Middle West in the 1930s, he stopped the performance by his company of Men Dancers and told the audience, "I have danced before the cowboys of Texas and the hillbillies of North Carolina, and I've never been subjected before to such a rude audience as this." He gave them further hell, continued the performance to rapt attention, and was given an ovation at the end. *Time* ran a photo of him in a one-piece bathing suit with one strap pulled down and a nipple bared. The caption read something to the effect that the cowboys and the hillbillies liked him.

Did *Time* have a personal grudge? Not at all. They felt, I found out by talking to a staff member, that Ted Shawn was a fraud, that he pretended to use profound themes—dancing to Bach, dancing to Plato, calling a number "an elemental rhythmus"—when what he turned up with was "circus." In fact, Emily Coleman, dance and music critic for the rival *Newsweek* Magazine, though sympathetic to his ideas for his ensemble of Men Dancers and even to much of his choreography, would groan when a primitive dance of fire found the men in silken capes walking along the stage and suddenly pulling open the capes to reveal scarlet linings and bodies bare except for silver jockstraps. Shawn would justify his whole approach with a battery of explanations, sometimes ethnic, sometimes otherwise, but the truth was that he was, and always had been, guilty of bad taste, especially in matters of costume.

His flamboyant style was already set in 1917 when there seemed to be a valid, promotional reason for the mixture of the serious and the popular. It was in the summer of 1917 that Ted created his first dances to two-part and three-part inventions and a four-voice fugue of Bach. These meticulously composed dance studies were a splendid contribution to that new genre which St. Denis, always the innovator, had originated. The term selected to describe those new choreographic areas was "music visualization."

St. Denis, while deeply—and honestly—admiring her famous contemporary and only rival, Isadora Duncan, felt that only Duncan, because of her great personal performing powers and magnetism, could get away with "interpreting" a major piece of music, say a symphony. A lesser dancer would be presumptuous to attempt it. But St. Denis sought and found a valid relationship between dance and music that had not been composed for dance, unlike some of Tchaikovsky's scores, which had been commissioned expressly for ballet use. St. Denis wished to relate a set piece of music to dance form, and it was her idea to have movement mirror the notes, the phrases, the dynamic intensities, the stresses, the moods, the styles, even the melodies, as well as the underlying rhythms of music. Thus "music visualizations" were added to the Denishawn repertory, and decades later, within the school of classical ballet, George Balanchine, the genius of ballet-making, won most of his fame for "pure" ballet works, nonnarrative creations which were simply extensions of musical sound into body substance, musical form into dance form— truly, "music visualizations."

Shawn went hungrily into the idea. St. Denis, as usual, dallied with it (and successfully) but got bored and moved on to new inventions. As she once told me, "I've actually invented a great many approaches to dance, but I've almost always left it to others to do something with my ideas." Ted worked hard on the Bach, and the inventions, fugues, and toccatas he choreographed later for his Men Dancers were so skillfully wrought that the music critic, Pitts Sanborn, wrote that if the scores of Bach, by some catastrophe should be lost, it would be possible to reconstruct them with considerable accuracy through the Shawn choreography. Whether this should be taken as a compliment to an artist or a recognition of a craftsman is for the viewer to decide. For me it represented the artist-craftsman at his cool best.

During the same summer Ted choreographed a dance which subsequently won him a popularity contest. It was made for a pupil, Mary Hay, later to star on Broadway as an actress, who wanted something "fierce" to dance. Ted took a John Philip Sousa piece called "The Red Man" (from a suite titled *Dwellers in the Western World*) and came up with a ritual rain dance which he named *Invocation to the Thunderbird*. He liked it so much that he subsequently adapted it for himself, and it became almost his trade mark, an American Indian dance of great virility, strength, athletic prowess, and intense sense of ritual.

A few summers later he made up a classroom exercise which called for the dancers to hold their bodies in contracted, flat positions as if they were bas-reliefs. It was simply a movement discipline for body control, but St. Denis was so impressed with it, she suggested he keep it as a solo. He did. He used music of Erik Satie—and was therefore the first choreographer to employ the music of an avant-garde composer whose works in concert had delighted him, and he cast it in terms of a Cretan ritual suggested by ancient bas-reliefs. He named it *Gnosienne* in an allusion to the ancient capital of Crete, Knossos (or Gnossos) and it too became an enduring Shawn favorite.

At the outset the matter of Ted's taste arose. His costume was brief, and the motif consisted of coils of material, rather like rubber tires, which were worn around his waist at the top of his trunks and around his thighs at the bottoms of his trunks. He also, at first, had the tire decor going between his legs. St. Denis took one look and realized that it was downright vulgar. She told me many years later, "Teddy was stubborn and I knew better than to tell him that the crotch tire was excessive and in bad taste. So I praised the costume, commented on the originality of the tires, and then hesitated, rather cleverly I thought, and said that something was wrong, but that I could not pin it down at once. After a moment I said, 'Ah, yes, I think I know. You have one tire too many. The one between the legs must go because it destroys the line of your legs, and your legs are so beautiful I just can't bear to see them impeded in any way.' It worked and I got the damn thing off him."

The summer of 1917 also recorded the arrival of Doris Humphrey to Denishawn. She had traveled all the way from Oak Park, Illinois, to study with the only serious dance artists, other than a handful of ballet teachers, she knew of in all of America. She had studied ballet and a kind of free dance, distantly related, perhaps, to Duncan's way and also to folk forms. She had a remarkable kinetic memory which enabled her, as a child, to see a Pavlova program once, memorize all of the dances, and reproduce them at church or town bazaars (for small payments) to the delight of her neighbors.

A decade later Doris would leave Denishawn to start an independent career with a later Denishawner, Charles Weidman, and to earn for herself recognition as the foremost choreographer in the field of America's modern dance. She was primarily a student, disciple, and favorite of Ruth St. Denis.

Martha Graham, who had grown up in nearby Santa Barbara and been swept into an unalterable life of dance when (like Ted himself) she first saw Ruth St. Denis dance in 1911, had hoped that her goddess would be her teacher when she came to Denishawn the summer before Doris. Her idol, however, found the strange little lady (she was past twenty) not at all compatible to her own tall, sinuous, lyrical style, and she pushed her off on Ted. During her years at Denishawn (until she left in 1923) Graham was chiefly a product of Shawn, although she came to dislike him intensely and to worship St. Denis even more deeply than ever, temporary rejection to one side.

Shawn gave Martha her first solo, *Serenata Morisca* (which he had choreographed earlier), appointed her an assistant teacher, and subsequently made her a national star by creating a dance drama on a passionate Toltec theme especially for her in a vaudeville tour which he himself arranged. The work was called *Xochitl*, and it was a triumph for Graham—Ted, in later tours, often danced the costar lead with her. But their temperaments clashed to the point of violence, and long after Martha had left Denishawn, she would say bluntly that he was no artist and he would classify her as "anti-Christ." Yet she owed the successful start of her career to him, and he owed several rewarding seasons of Denishawn-originated performances to her vivid and popular presence.

World War I was now involving the United States, and Ted was determined to enlist in the army. In his usual practical way he prepared for the move. Ruth would take Doris and some of the dancers on a vaudeville tour and would use her great prestige to sell Liberty Bonds. Ted set to work creating three short ballets for the vaudeville circuit. These were scenically elaborate, inventive, and appealing productions. One was suggested by the zodiac and emerged as a sort of astral ballet. Another was a rousing Maori dance, and the third was a *tableau vivant* extended into dance and suggested by Botticelli's famous *La Primavera*. Bookings were arranged so that the Denishawn dancers would be occupied for many months and the Denishawn name would be kept alive.

Ted, fortunately, was stationed at nearby Camp Kearny at the Officers Training School. Martha taught for him, and he dashed into Los Angeles on weekend leaves to conduct as many classes as possible. His enlistment was for the ambulance corps, and he never left Camp Kearny for the short duration of America's war involvement.

He even managed to get away to San Francisco long enough to offer an entire church service in dance form at the Interdenominational Church there. He had, much earlier, included "The Twenty-third Psalm" in his repertory, but this was the first time in church history that an entire service was conceived in dance. It was a Shawn innovation, later to be adopted in related guises by St. Denis in the last decades of her life when she focused upon programs dealing with dance and religion.

By 1917 Ted Shawn was sufficiently famous to cause newspaper headlines when he enlisted, and even cartoons, such as one showing a major cowboy star and Ted, dressed in a leopard skin, leaping along as stretcher bearers.

Nineteen fifteen (with the founding of Denishawn), 1916, and 1917 were historic years with foundations laid, dancers discovered, choreographic innovations born which were to affect not only the course of dance but of the theater itself. Part of the swift events of 1917 saw the enforced separation of St. Denis and Shawn. She visited him, whenever her tours permitted, at Camp Kearny amid attendant publicity, and the two performed for patriotic causes when they could.

But Ruth was off on her own, relieved to be free of Shawn's attempted domination and his insistence on disciplines, and by the time the armistice came on November 11, 1918, new patterns had been set. For a while he would run not Denishawn School, which went through a suspended period, but a revived Ted Shawn school of dance. The two would work and experiment separately—he continuing his enormously successful art-dance productions for vaudeville—until 1922 (except for occasional joint appearances where the two magically linked names were demanded by managers) when Denishawn was reborn, both as school and company. A great burst of activity and creativity would propel them to the peak of the Denishawn Age, an era in dance unequaled in the years before and, in the sense of historic context, unmatched for uniqueness in the years beyond.

7

With this pause in the career of Ted Shawn, I find myself experiencing a curious need to pause also, to look back on my own feelings about this remarkable—good and bad—man.

In reading this narrative as I have written it up to this point and reading too the cartons of notes and essays and sketches I have jotted down, I find that, in retrospect, I don't seem to like Ted Shawn very much. He has come out on these pages thus far as a skillful opportunist in certain respects, a self-centered individual with a relentless ambition and an artist of sometimes questionable taste. I never meant it to come out this way, although I knew his faults well, but somehow it has. It is not quite as corny as "the truth will out," but writing the biography has made me want to assess the man in a new light. In his lifetime I believed myself to be very fond of him and, as a critic, protective of his position in dance history. Indeed, I believed then and do now that he was one of the most important individuals in the annals of dance, although his stature as an artist was always under debate and his treatment of others was more often shocking than not.

Stuart Sebastian, a university student and a young choreographer who has studied, under an off-campus university instructional program, with me, never saw Shawn and knew him only as a major name in the story of dance. I asked him what he wanted to know about this dancing ancestor of his. He replied, "How did he treat people—his dancers, his friends, the ones that worked for him?"

He treated me (first as a sort of protégé and later as a friend and writer who tried to report fairly on his many works) very well indeed. I think he was genuinely fond of me. Why, then, does so much that is unflattering emerge on these pages? For all I have written is quite true. I have pondered, and I realize what he possessed in abundant measure was instant charm. He could charm anybody.

Mary Watkins, the first dance critic in America (she was appointed to the job on the *New York Herald Tribune* in 1928), reminisced about the major figures in American dance in an interview I did with her in 1974, a few weeks before her death at eighty-six. She had something pithy, and not always flattering, to say about St. Denis, Graham, Humphrey, and others. But when I came to ask about Ted Shawn, she smiled almost rapturously and said, "He was appealing to any woman. Oh, my yes!"

When he stopped briefly in Chapel Hill, that first time I met him, to visit one of his former dancers, now our teacher, Phoebe Barr, her worship had already brushed off on us. As I say, he didn't look very much like the glamorous man some of us had seen on stage in concert. But he was most gracious to all of us. He was especially impressed with my roommate, Foster Fitz-Simons, who was the best dancer in our group, and later engaged him as a member of his Men Dancers group. He was very pleasant to me. And I told him that I wanted to be a writer about dance rather than a dancer. He was very pleased about that, for John Martin, the dance critic of the *New York Times* (who had been appointed shortly after Mary Watkins had begun criticism for the rival *Tribune*), had treated him and St. Denis unmercifully in his columns while supporting the new efforts of the Denishawn rebels, Graham, Humphrey, Weidman, and their associates. I remember sitting on the floor at his feet at Phoebe's house and how he leapt at the notion that here, perhaps, was a potential dance critic who would "tell the truth," as he described his preeminent place in American dance.

In later years he would always say that because I did not have the ideal dancer's build—I was short and tended to be stocky—although I had a really great jump!—he had suggested dance criticism for my career. This was not so, for I came from a family of writers and, before discovering dance, had concentrated on music and drama studies with the idea of becoming a critic of one or both of those arts. When I came upon dance, well before I met Ted Shawn, I had said to Foster, "I've found it. I'm going to be a dance critic."

Shawn, when he invited Foster to join his company, also invited me to study one summer at his Jacob's Pillow dance farm in the

Berkshire Hills of Massachusetts and, if I did well, join his company. I would have tried it for experience only, but although Foster was graduating, I had another year of college and, after much thought and discussion with my parents, I decided to finish school. I'm glad I did.

Foster wrote to me after he had been with Shawn for a few months and, thinking I would be joining him at the dance camp, issued a warning. We had thought of Ted Shawn as something of a god. He wrote that he had become disillusioned and he didn't want me to go through the same depressing experience. For he discovered, as he put it, that Ted Shawn was not only not a god but that he was a very petty man. That's what one of his featured dancers thought of him.

Intellectually he had a running battle with Foster that he did not have with other members of the troupe. As at Denishawn he loved to select books and articles and read aloud to his young disciples. He would announce that this was good and that was bad, something was right and the other was wrong, and expected, even demanded, that everyone agree with him. Foster would not. He would simply speak up at the dining table or while sunbathing at lunchtime and say, "I don't agree." That was heresy. No one had a choice. You were supposed to agree. Foster obeyed all dance instructions, but although Shawn controlled his dance action, he did not control Foster's mind.

He tried the same tactics with me. I was the second maverick in this period of his life. I listened to him, learned from him, respected him, but when I disagreed with him, I said so.

On the other hand he was remarkably generous to his dancers and absolutely paternal about their well-being. In the days when theater unions were just beginning to exert some influence and when the dance union was weak (the American Guild of Musical Artists, AGMA, is the dancers union), Shawn paid his Men Dancers from 1933 to 1940 higher wages than the union was asking. Furthermore, he guaranteed them year-round maintenance, something that no union asked or ever got from an employer. When he disbanded the company after seven years as World War II came along, he gave each a parcel of land at Jacob's Pillow or a nice cash sum as a bountiful "thank you."

Even if he tried to control the minds of his dancers, he never invaded their privacy. Many of the boys built their own cabins deep in the woods on the Jacob's Pillow acreage. Since they were at close quarters for most of the year—sometimes 150 one-night stands—they needed privacy desperately. Ted never visited a cabin unless asked. He never spied on any of his boys. He never quizzed them on their private lives. He demanded that they be gentlemen in public, comport themselves with dignity, and never, ever show one touch of effeminacy. His battle after all was to prove the masculinity of dance.

In his readings he touched upon the Greek ideal of male love but he never tried to convert anyone to homosexuality. He himself, obviously, was bisexual. Most of his men were heterosexual, but a few of his dancers were either homo or bi. Neither did he himself court any of them. Unlike St. Denis he was not at all promiscuous. A permanent relationship, starting with Ruth but continuing with males, was all he ever sought. Indeed, if she had been faithful to him, it is possible, if not probable, that he would never have elected the homosexual way of life in spite of his own ambivalence.

When his dancers were ill, he tended them like a mother-father figure. Once, on tour, there was a terrible automobile accident, and some of the boys were hospitalized. Shawn, who had been in a different car, was unhurt. But he rushed to the hospital and held hands and heads while surgeons were sewing up wounds. He stayed by the bedsides until curtain time and then he and Barton Mumaw, the junior star of his troupe, threw together a program of solos and adapted duets so that the show could go on. He was genuine in his concern for his boys' well-being, but he absolutely adored the situation. He wrote me about his own performance that night in a personal letter describing the accident and body repairs in gory detail and wound up with a comment on his own performance: "People said I had never been so electrifying!"

He had various ways of treating people who disagreed with him, crossed him, or whom he did not need any more. The way he eased Hazel Wallack and Norma Gould out of his life was just the starter. His recurrent term for anyone who did not do his bidding was "disloyal." It was as cut-and-dried as that. But when someone bucked him whom he did not wish to get rid of, he would invent excuses for him. Once he was furious with the independent-minded, temperamental La Meri, one of the great ethnic dance experts of this century and with whom, it was said, he was in love (in the 1940s). He did not throw her out of Jacob's Pillow because he needed her as head of his ethnic dance wing (she drew pupils) and as a popular performer. He told me in one session, "She's been impossible, but, of course, she isn't really responsible for her behavior. She's having change of life, you know, and all women are unpredictable then." I told this to La Meri and she roared with laughter. She was having no such difficulties and simply remarked that since she knew his ego, he would have to find an excuse for her because he could not possibly admit that he was a son of a bitch.

With Myra Kinch, the head of his modern dance wing, he was sweet for years. He told me that she did not draw pupils to Jacob's Pillow as well as some others might do but that he was "loyal" to her. The truth was that as he grew older and his performing limitations became considerable and his choreographic invention began to wane fast, she was useful in creating vehicles for him that showed him off to his best advantage. She did a work based on King Lear for him, another about an old gypsy king and the like, but once he had had a mild heart attack and no longer needed her for dance pieces she was eased out of Jacob's Pillow. This he described to me as "releasing Myra from her obligations—without rancor—so that she could do other things." What, he didn't really care.

But he was equally quick to come to the aid of the distressed, in tangible terms as well as with sympathy. When one of his Denishawn-trained dancers, Miriam Winslow, had been "disloyal" to him, he let her know, but when her brother died suddenly and she appealed to him for help in filling a concert date for her, he dropped everything and did a solo recital as a pinch hitter. She paid him, of course, but he didn't *have* to replace her, a far less famous student, if he hadn't felt for her needs. He never forgave her, however, for hiring Foster Fitz-Simons away from him to become her partner. "About the Foster-Mimi thing," he wrote me, "I am *not* happy."

He was impressed by famous people, by royalty, by the powerful he met during his long career, but he was never a snob. He was as attentive to a student with a problem or a fan at the stage door as he was with the president of a corporation or a great star of the theater. He had time for everyone. Like a benevolent despot he cared for the less fortunate, and no one was ever barred from his presence. He felt a great duty to his public and a genuine love for these unidentified thousands. I remember once joining him in his dressing room at the Washington Irving High School in New York City at the close of a long, arduous tour. He was sweating, the heavy makeup was still on, and he had just put on his white terry-cloth bathrobe, a sort of priestly trade-mark, when there was a knock on the door and someone said, "Mr. Shawn, there are people here to see you." He slumped for a moment and turned to me: "I wish I didn't have to go out there and smile and say thank you and sign autographs and do all the things I'm supposed to do. I wish they'd all go away." He paused, "But the day they don't come, I'll die." And he went out and smiled and pressed hands and said, "Of course I remember you, how nice of you to come to say hello," and "Oh, yes, I remember that performance in Slippery Rock, how good of you to remember it too," and on and on until every autograph was signed.

Ted Shawn knew his job. He did it with irresistible charm.

His generosity, however, was tempered with narrow-mindedness. He wanted the men's group at the Pillow not only to work as hard as he demanded (and he worked at menial tasks alongside them), but he also wanted them to be happy. On free evenings he would permit the boys and girl visitors (or summer female students) to have parties in the big studio. But he hated jazz and felt it was decadent, although he danced to it in a commentary on a demoralized era. One night the boys and their girls were dancing to hot jazz in the studio. They were playing it too loud. Suddenly the door opened and there stood Ted Shawn. He was wearing his snowy white bathrobe. His hair was perfectly groomed. One of the boys later told me he thought he had put on a very subtle stage makeup. He looked at the now silent group and said, "You have desecrated my temple." Then he fainted. He was borne to his room by members of the troupe. It never happened again.

But then you would find him, side by side with his boys and scholarship students, working on the rough road to the Pillow, repairing stone walls, planting the vegetable garden, and even enlarging the pit for the two-seater outhouse (which he himself never used).

He was a complex, contradictory, controversial man. He once said that one had to be a great person in order to be a great artist. Some years later I happened to write an article in which I said that I had never met a great star who was very nice, that they were all monsters, much as Deems Taylor, the music critic, had described Richard Wagner, adding that perhaps with genius it didn't matter how dreadful a person was. Ted read my article and complimented me on it. He added that the new generation of artists was guilty of what I had said, and wasn't it too bad that they could not emulate the standards of his generation. He meant that he was the one exception to what I had written.

Near the end of his life he went into a tirade about people who had been "disloyal" to him, triggered by the most recent defection. As he finished, he looked at me and said, "Well, I guess I'm a son of a bitch." "Yes you are," I replied. Then he burst into tears. "How could you say that about me?" he sobbed. "I didn't say it," I replied. "You said it and everyone knows that you insist that everyone agree with you and I'm simply agreeing with you." It was bitchy of me but even I would get weary of his endless attacks on those who didn't do as he commanded.

I may brag that I fixed him once for fair on the Martha Graham question, which haunted him. He had done a spectacular job of taking her whole approach to dance and all her dance creations and her statements and her behavior to prove that she was "anti-Christ." Then he would launch into a harangue about how she always said she was Ruth's pupil and not his when everyone, including Ruth, knew that Martha was a Shawn product and that without him she would have amounted to nothing. I fixed him with an eye and said, "Ted, you can't have it both ways. Either she is a great, great dancer and you showed her the way, or she is anti-Christ for exactly the same reason, your influence. You accept her as yours or agree with those who say she was never yours." He was flustered for about the only time I have ever seen it happen. He blurted out, "Well, of course she's mine. She's, well, of course I trained her, well . . . naturally I admire her extravagantly. Of course I taught her and did everything for her. Of course she's a genius." We had no further Graham diatribes after that.

So what I have said here—and I shall say more—is what Ted Shawn was like. It is, as you can see, difficult to say whether you like him or not. Perhaps one's feelings about him are best described by a viewpoint which one of Ruth St. Denis's closest friends held about her: "It is impossible to like Miss Ruth. She really isn't likeable at all. She isn't a bit nice as a person. But it is possible to love her. That's all you can do with someone like that."

I think that is probably the way I feel about Ted Shawn. When I finish writing this book covering his life as I have researched it and forty years of that life as I played a part in it, I shall probably find out. "How did he treat people?" as Sebastian asked. The answer must be there.

Certainly he was faced with the difficult job of treating me as a critic and also as a friend. I don't believe he ever divorced the two, especially if his own work or something he presented as an impresario was involved. In 1938, when I had been a critic on the *Boston Herald* for about a year and a half, he wrote me a long, long letter in which he said, "I know I'm expecting something of you that should not be expected this early. You are growing, and that is fine, but you are also passing through in your critical career the stages analogous to the measles and the mumps in childhood."

What he really wanted of me was a critic who would treat him, in print, like a personal press agent would treat him in a press release he had paid for. A classic example of his thinking on this score came to me in a long letter (1939) which had been triggered by a review in which I had panned a new solo of his, *The Whirlwind*. Here's how he treated me in response to my critical treatment of him: "Your review was never a 'sore' point. I was just terribly let down . . . it was a dull and stupid review, no matter what anyone else may say, and impossible for me to use in any way—which I thought I had a right to expect. . . . Even if you're right about the 'Whirlwind' it is unjustly disproportionate to let that color the whole review, and spoil it entirely for me to reproduce. Had you stressed the good things and merely mentioned that you didn't care for that one solo, in passing in a closing sentence, it still would have served your purpose and mine. But you must go your own way and learn your lessons, the hard way, by making these mistakes, I suppose."

But his treatment of the "naughty" boy did not work. If it had, I would have been of no use to myself, to dance reviewing, to him. He came, in time, to treat me with a little more respect and, more important, to let me reserve myself for the function of a dance critic. But he kept trying to induce a critic to write like a friend. For my part I tried to separate the two. I treated him as a performer-choreographer-director in my reviews, as a friend in my letters and conversations. I always treated him with respect.

Above: Elmer Ellsworth Shawn, Ted's father, as a bridegroom, and Mary Lee Booth, the girl who was to become Mrs. E. E. Shawn. *Below:* Which was her favorite son?
Left, Arnold Booth Shawn, high school athlete, Ted's older brother.
Right, Edwin Myers (Ted) Shawn, high school scholar.

The "shocking" pose: Ted and his
teacher-partner-fiancée, Hazel Wallack.
Denver, 1910.

Right, Ted and his second partner,
Norma Gould, successful in *Tango Teas*
in Los Angeles. 1911.

Rembrandt.

Ted and Norma in search of dance "art." A semi-ballet lift in *La Danse d'Amour*, a French love waltz; *below left*, in a semi-Oriental courtship; *below right*, as teachers of courses from *Nature and Barefoot* to *Choreographic Drama*.

Norma Gould and Ted Shawn

INTERPRETIVE AND CLASSIC
DANCERS
AND TEACHERS OF INTERPRETIVE
AND CLASSIC DANCING

STUDIO, 1615 GEORGIA STREET
LOS ANGELES, CAL.
PHONE, 22249

Photos: Mojonier, Los Angeles.

The onetime theology student dances an entire church service for the first time. International Church, San Francisco, 1917.
Right, Ted in early solos: *top,* sullen, well-dressed refinement; *center,* a daringly semi-draped "Bacchus."
Bottom, Ruth St. Denis and Ted Shawn in the "commercial" ballroom dances she detested. This one made history: in a contest for a title, the winner suggested "Denishawn" Rose Mazurka. The dance was forgotten, the coined name came to designate an era in dance history. 1915.

Poster for the first mammoth Denishawn production: *A Dance Pageant of Egypt, Greece and India.* Martha Graham made her dance debut as an Egyptian priestess.

The *Pageant* also permitted Ted to create his first all-male group dance, "Pyrrhic Warriors."
Below: In 1918, Cecil B. de Mille asked Ted, then in the U.S. Army, to do a dream
sequence with Gloria Swanson in a movie. As a faun, he chased her, caught her, and
kissed her for twenty-eight seconds for a fee of $500. In 1961, he repeated the kiss (free).
In 1971, Swanson (72) kissed Ted on his last birthday (80).

Ruth St. Denis and Ted Shawn at the height of their joint career an *Algerian Dance.*

Left: The young Ted Shawn with his world-famous bride, Ruth St. Denis: partner? wife? mother substitute?

In 1920, Ted created *Xochitl*, a Toltec ballet, as a starring vehicle for Martha Graham. She danced it first with Robert Gorham (illustrated), then with the young Charles Weidman and finally with Shawn himself. It served her in vaudeville and in the Denishawn concert company for two years.

Below, Denishawn on a U.S. tour, with St. Denis and Shawn as co-engineers. "Name" dancers in the pose: *fourth from right*, Jeordie Graham (Martha's sister, who inherited her roles); *fifth*, Pauline Lawrence (she became Mrs. José Limón); *seventh*, Doris Humphrey, to become modern dance's major choreographer; *ninth*, Charles Weidman, the other half of the yet-to-come Humphrey-Weidman Dancers.

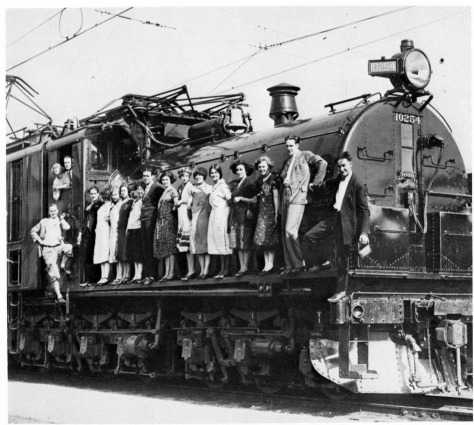

Gigantic posters proclaimed the dance—even the theatrical—preeminence of Ruth St. Denis, Ted Shawn, and their Denishawn Dancers in almost every town and city throughout the United States and London, and for nearly two years in the Orient.

Right, Gnosienne, a Cretan dance in which Ted used avant-garde movement to avant-garde music (by Satie) in a costume saved from becoming too "avant" (by R. St. D.). 1919.

Below, Ted tried his skill at Spanish dance early; after studies in Spain, he transformed himself into one of the best of the non-Spanish exponents of Spanish dancing.

When his wife spent a fortune producing her Babylonian ballet, *Ishtar of the Seven Gates*, Ted countered by putting a full Indian pueblo on stage as a setting for his Hopi Indian Eagle Dance in *Feather of the Dawn*. 1923.

Below left, America's most celebrated male dancer interprets *The Cosmic Dance of Shiva*, India's Nataraja, Lord of Dancing. 1926.

Below right, "I will dance nude," Ted vowed. He did in a cool, tasteful plastique accepted nervously by American audiences (1923), cheered by Oriental audiences (1925–1926) —*The Death of Adonis*.

In 1920, *Frohsinn* was mainly a warm-up study in free-style, barefoot ballet for Ted. A decade later, it received forty-seven curtain calls in Munich.

Below left, Idyll—the end of Denishawn, the last duet Ruth St. Denis and Ted Shawn created for themselves as heads of Denishawn. They were already separated as husband and wife when they performed this love duet for thousands of fans at Lewisohn Stadium, 1929. Two years later, a final Lewisohn contract was filled and Denishawn ceased to be.

Below: At forty, Ted begins a new career in the all-male, Spartan surroundings of his colonial farm in the Berkshire hills of Massachusetts. The Greek ideal of the dancing athlete is celebrated.

For the forty years at Jacob's Pillow, the boss dancer works side by side with his students in non-dance labors.
Below: The "dancing athletes." Ted Shawn and his Men Dancers (1933–1940) in the Bach "Three-Part Invention," a music visualization. Wilbur McCormack, Frank Delmar, Barton Mumaw, Fred Hearn, Shawn, Frank Overlees, Harry Coble, John Delmar, John Schubert.

Dwight Godwin.

Above left, Barton Mumaw, first soloist of the men's group, in *The French Sailor*, one of many tremendously popular solos created for him by Shawn.

Above: Virtuosity, maturity, and spiritual ecstasy in a long-lasting audience favorite, Ted Shawn's continuously whirling solo, *Mevlevi Dervish*.

Left, Mumaw and McCormack—the very essence of Shawn's concept of dances of prowess for American men.

Dance festivals succeed the era of the men dancers at Jacob's Pillow. An all-star collection includes England's Anton Dolin, Doris Humphrey (a visitor), Alexander Alexay (composer-pianist), Shawn, St. Denis, the great prima ballerina Alicia Markova, and Charles Weidman (a visitor here; he returned some years later to dance at the Pillow as the Humphrey-Weidman breach with Denishawn slowly relaxed). 1941.

Below left, Shawn and St. Denis—he in his sixties, she nearing eighty—memories in movement.

Below right, Shawn as King Lear in *Sundered Majesty*, a work tailored to his age by Myra Kinch (Ophelia).

Radford Bascome.

John Lindquist.

Shawn at seventy-six on his beloved stage at Jacob's Pillow dances for the last time his great solo, *O Brother Sun and Sister Moon: A Study of St. Francis*, created in 1931 and described as "a dance in dynamic stillness."

Below left: On their fiftieth wedding anniversary in 1964, Ruth St. Denis and Ted Shawn danced together for the last time in a new duet, a gestural dance of spirits of the upper air created by Shawn. He was nearly seventy-four and she about eighty-seven when this photo was taken.

Below right: Late in life, Shawn turned to wood carving. He called this one "Flying Icarus," and of his work he said, "I have no illusions about my being a sculptor—but I do have FUN, and no matter what *I* do the *wood* is still beautiful."

Louis Peres.

Right: Two or three months before he died he went to see a different kind of dancer, tap star Ruby Keeler, in the last Broadway show he was to see, *No, No, Nanette.*

A last favorite portrait.

Frank Derbas.

8

Ruth St. Denis did not treat her husband very well.

Understandably, during his brief military career, they could not see much of each other. She made a visit to the officers training camp, he was able to teach in Los Angeles during many of his weekends, but she was off on tour most of the time. Along with other great stars of the day, Mary Pickford and Douglas Fairbanks among them, she used her great prestige to sell Liberty Bonds across the country, and through her vaudeville earnings to set an example for others by buying a large quota of bonds herself. She began to savor independence from her ambitious, organizational-minded husband.

Her first tour, beginning in January 1918, was primarily a solo affair. Margaret Loomis, from Denishawn, would dance two or three numbers, but for the rest it was a St. Denis recital. Louis Horst was along as musical director. This was a West, Midwest, and Canadian tour. In the summer she staged the dances and appeared in *The Light of Asia* at a theosophical center in Los Angeles and subsequently danced at the Greek Theater in the Gluck opera, *Orfeo ed Euridice*. By November she was on the road again, this time for a coast-to-coast vaudeville tour with four girls (Doris Humphrey, Betty Horst, Edna Malone, Pearl Wheeler) and Louis Horst again. The vaudeville circuit was called Pantages, one of the biggest in America, and it was on Pantages tours that both she and Shawn, separately and together, made money. The recital field, which they both preferred because they could do exactly as they pleased and need not share billing with other acts, was more precarious financially.

It was on one such engagement that St. Denis had time to write her husband: "Darling, when you reach that point when you realize that your destiny is to serve me and my career, subordinate to me at

all times and in all ways, you will finally reach some happiness."
This became a recurrent theme in their marriage and joint career. At
first it hurt him deeply, then it angered him, it continuously irritated
him, and in the last decades of his life it would haunt him so
thoroughly that he would come to believe that not only St. Denis
but also Martha and Doris and Charles and everyone who opposed
him saw him only as a servitor. And, indeed, he was an unhappy
man not because he did not obey her but because her continuing
demand filled him with self-doubts that he dared not show the
world.

The uxorial and professional demand for dominance was destruc-
tive to his inner being, but it could not stop his personal drive for
recognition and success. While St. Denis was on tour and he was
still in the army or, later, running a school and company without
her, he pursued his career methodically and unrelentingly. While at
officers training he got a call from Cecil B. De Mille asking him to
do a fast movie job. Since he was being trained to be "an officer and
a gentleman" and since the job called for him to shed most of his
clothes, embrace a young lady horizontally and kiss her twenty-eight
seconds, he was not certain that the two were compatible, but five
hundred dollars for four hours' work was not to be resisted.

The scene in the movie, *Why Change Your Wife?*, starring Gloria
Swanson, was a vision in which Miss Swanson was to encounter
Wealth, Pleasure, Love. Wealth and Pleasure had been shot. De
Mille said he could not shoot Love without Ted, a friend and col-
league who had staged dances for earlier De Mille films. Shawn was
a faunlike creature basking on a rock playing pipes of Pan. Gloria, as
a nymph, appears. The faun chases her, stretches her out on a rock,
reaches for a handy bunch of grapes, and squeezes them into her
mouth. This is followed by a kiss carefully clocked, as Shawn recalled, at twenty-eight seconds.

The first rehearsals were done with Miss Swanson's understudy.
The bunch of grapes contained tiny sponges filled with Welch's
grape juice so that the cascade would show. It nearly drowned the
understudy. Ultimately the ex-divinity student convinced De Mille
that God knew what he was up to in matters of grapes, and so Miss
Swanson received only the juice from the bunch itself and the extended kiss, announcing that it was "delicious," whether the juice or

kiss or both she did not specify. When he told the story to the great actress Ethel Barrymore some years later, the celebrated stage star growled in her deep voice, "Kiss Gloria Swanson? Five hundred dollars? Ted, my dear, not half enough!"

But Ted never forgot the occasion of his movie with one of the most famous movie queens of all time. Years later, when Swanson was acting in a play at the Berkshire Playhouse near Shawn's Jacob's Pillow Dance Festival, they reenacted the pose for publicity, and on the occasion of Shawn's eightieth birthday, at a huge celebration at the Dance Collection of the New York Public Library, Miss Swanson, playing on Broadway in *Butterflies Are Free*, arrived at the star-studded gathering with a small bunch of grapes—she swore it was her usual lunch!—fortuitously present in her handbag. Shawn was very ill—actually he was nearing the end of his life—and midway in the celebration he asked the curator of the Dance Collection, Genevieve Oswald, if he could rest in her office and receive treatment from his therapist who helped alleviate some of the discomforts of emphysema. Miss Swanson, one of the many who had spoken words of tribute, was about to leave. I asked her if she would stay a moment longer. She agreed and I rushed to Shawn to see if he felt well enough to reenact the grapes scene for the occasion. I urged Miss Oswald to get the old 1918 still from the files, and Shawn, dismissing his genuine fatigue, sat next to Swanson, held the old photo, and carried on happily while two photographers shot the reunion with the very weary old gentleman and the still glamorous Swanson, past seventy herself. An effort you say? No, therapy. Swanson, the grapes, the cameras did more than any therapist could do.

Soon after the movie for De Mille the war came to an abrupt end, Shawn was discharged, and with his five hundred dollars headed for his wife, who was playing a full week in Detroit (December 9 to 15, 1918). From her letters he knew that the reunion was not going to be as easy as the Swanson kiss, but he had no notion what the week would bring—the near termination of a marriage, the temporary end of Denishawn.

The talks and battles, arguments and tears continued, along with the demands of two-a-day vaudeville, for seven days. St. Denis announced that she was not a "robot." She shouted that she wanted nothing to do with a company and a school. She wept that school, company, even the partnership had been forced upon her. That it was he who made her repeat dances endlessly during endless tours of one-night stands, thus killing her art and stifling her soul. This theme was to be played again and again during the length of their joint career—in 1918, however, it served to strangle Denishawn for a little more than three years.

Ted returned to Los Angeles and saw to the closing of the big Denishawn School in the house at Westlake Park. He retained a smaller house (on Sixth Street), and it was here that he and Martha Graham taught classes and from which he picked dancers to send out on Denishawn concert engagements or for vaudeville acts. Ted taught the professionals, or would-be pros, and Martha the business girls in night classes. Calls for Denishawn dancers were usually supplied on the basis of which dancer fit an existing costume for the requested routine. This was vaudeville production time for Ted Shawn. He created dances—routines they were called—for soloists, duos, trios, but he also staged major dance productions which would serve as the star act in a vaudeville show or, better yet, be presented as the "class act."

Every imaginable form of entertainment was to be found in vaudeville. The great ballerina Anna Pavlova and the great actress Sarah Bernhardt thought nothing of sharing a bill with trained seals, jugglers, contortionists, circus freaks. Pavlova, Bernhardt, Shawn, St. Denis, and others of their stature were the acts which gave a "high-class" stamp to a vaudeville show. These were "class act" artists as distinct from burlesque comics, singers of popular songs or jugglers.

I remember my mother taking me in from the country to see vaudeville at that Mecca for vaudevillians, the Palace on New York's Broadway. Vaudeville meant entertainment long before television was dreamed of and when radio had just about been invented. Once Mother and I saw the great actor Maurice Schwartz in a scene from Shakespeare's *The Merchant of Venice*. Schwartz was, I believe, the finest Shylock of his day. On the same bill—or at least on a similar one—I saw a vaudeville act based on the gimmick of a dentist giving laughing gas (much used by dentists in the 1920s) to a patient. The patient, a very pretty girl with an infectious and varied laugh pattern, simply laughed throughout the act. That's all there was to it. Twenty-five or thirty years later, when vaudeville returned to the

Palace (decades after vaudeville had presumably died), I saw the act again. The two performers were now white-haired. The act, however, was unchanged.

Ted's first "class-act" production was *Julnar of the Sea*, an elaborate ballet based on a fairy tale. It opened in 1919 and played the Pantages circuit for two years. There were eleven dancers, men and women, including Lillian Powell as the principal, and Horst as musical director. There was a narrator also. (One of the replacement narrators was the same Honoria "Patsy" Donner who had been St. Denis's best friend during the Belasco days after the turn of the century.)

The second major production for vaudeville was the ballet created especially for Martha. It was the Aztec-Toltec production, *Xochitl*, which was premiered in 1921 and toured for two years, first with Robert Gorham in support of Graham, then Charles Weidman, and, subsequently in concert presentations, with Shawn. The third big vaudeville production was *Les Mystères Dionysiaques* in which Shawn himself took to the road, heading a cast of thirteen. All three were lavishly costumed and mounted with elaborate sets and scenery. This production approach was later to become a Denishawn trademark, and it served to make Ted Shawn, along with St. Denis and Denishawn, one of the most popular theatrical attractions in America. At that period the public could take art dance or leave it alone, preferably the latter, but Shawn, in these three vaudeville ballets and, subsequently, in Denishawn stagings, gave the public not so much dance as a show.

By nature Ted Shawn was flamboyant. As a child he had liked to dress up and he had been affected by the showmanship of vaudeville, almost the only form of theater he knew. In later years he never downgraded vaudeville. Both he and St. Denis, reminiscing about the past, would say, "In vaudeville, you had thirty seconds—no more—to get your audience, and if you missed in that period, you'd never get them. And it's true of art too. Today's dancers ought to learn that."

The trappings of theater, extravagant costumes, and exotic themes certainly appealed to young Ted, the novice choreographer, perhaps as a subconscious rebellion against the austerity of Methodism, against the drabness of standard life in Middle America.

He wanted to give the public, in vaudeville or in concert, a good show because he himself liked a good show and, deeper, because he wanted to be liked, to be popular. Still, he was not a superficial man, although he occasionally seemed to employ superficially slick exteriors. He was totally serious about the art of dancing and wholly dedicated, but just as he had admired Dr. Riesner and his highly theatrical approach to preaching, who, with lighted signs on the church lawn, enticed the public to divine services, Shawn felt that he must do the same in dance. Give them, the public, the divine message of dance, the sublime art, but get the public to accept it by using whatever splashy come-ons were necessary. Besides, in his mind, the profundity of a Promethean errand and the blaze of Promethean fire were not antithetical.

The only continuity of Denishawn at this point was maintained through Ted. As the school grew, he moved it to larger quarters in Los Angeles's Grand Street and called it the Ted Shawn Studio. In smaller letters, it said Denishawn Productions. This and the occasional joint appearances of the two stars were all that was left of Denishawn until 1922. When bookers insisted on the team, they reunited briefly, but St. Denis was primarily concerned with her concert dances. Among her ventures was a program of dance, music, and poetry (she had fallen in love with a young actor who did the narration) which she took on tour of the West Coast. She also borrowed some dancers from the Shawn studio and choreographed a dance to Schubert's *Unfinished Symphony*. The unique approach she employed she termed synchoric orchestra. The principle was that for each instrument in the orchestra there was a dancer or group of dancers who moved only when that instrument (or blocks of the same instrument, such as cellos) played. Many years later, in the 1930s, Ted used the synchoric concept with great success in Mozart's *Symphony in G Minor*, which he choreographed for his Men Dancers.

St. Denis and her concert dancers performed numbers to Chopin, Debussy, Schubert (the Schubert *Impromptu* remained a popular St. Denis solo for many years as did Doris Humphrey's *Soaring* to music of Schumann), Brahms, Bach. Some of the dances in the St. Denis repertory were choreographed by Shawn. There were some Bach in-

ventions here, and years later, in revised form, they served as a
brilliant and most successful part of the Men Dancers programs.

Ted did part of St. Denis's poetry tours with her. On these occasions they ended a program of danced poetry (this was St. Denis's
first major effort with the poems of India's great Rabindranath
Tagore and other Indian poets) with the popular *Egyptian Suite*,
stemming from Ruth's pre-Shawn *Egypta* and their later joint choreographies on Egyptian themes.

An acting stint augmented their dance schedule during this period
when the two starred in a play (not a danced play) in San Francisco.
It was written by Charles Caldwell Dobie and was called *Ramati:
Seed of the Lotus*. St. Denis herself had inspired the play. As a child
she had read *The Idyll of the White Lotus*, an allegory by Mabel Collins
about a youth of ancient Egypt who was a mystic and had a vision of
the Lady of the Lotus. St. Denis retold the story to Dobie, a novelist
and author of *San Francisco Tales*, and he came up with a drama based
upon it. It was produced by the Players Club of San Francisco, and
although it was not successful, it served as an example of the sort of
mystical drama which St. Denis always wanted for herself and never
succeeded in finding.

Ramati was done in 1920, and it was to be the last of her acting ad-
ventures for almost twenty years. Although she had been primarily a
dancer in the pre-*Radha* shows produced by David Belasco from 1899
to 1904, the roles also entailed some acting. She was, by her own admission in her diaries, envious of the Belasco star, Mrs. Leslie Carter, whom she supported in both *Zaza* and *Dubarry* at the turn of the
century, and when she herself approached ninety and dancing was
no longer easy, she used to tell me that she would like to return to
acting in one of Mrs. Carter's great roles. Indeed, in her eighties, she
had acted in *The Madwoman of Chaillot* and drove the cast to the
breakdown point because she couldn't remember her lines.

Ramati, then, was an understandable departure from dance for
her, and it was logical that she should drag her nonactor husband
along with her. Earlier, in 1918 while Ted was in military service,
she had participated in a dramatization of *The Light of Asia*, produced
by the Theosophical Institute of Hollywood and starring the popular
Shakespearean actor, Walter Hampden, as The Buddha. In this particular drama, however, St. Denis did not speak but danced the

vision scene as a solo and, with some Denishawn Dancers, the temptation scene.

Between *The Light of Asia* and *Ramati* came *Miriam, Sister of Moses* (1919), written especially for St. Denis by Constance Smedley and Maxwell Armstrong and presented at the Greek Theater in Berkeley. It was Ted's first professional acting job and, except for *Ramati*, his last until, as an elderly gentleman he returned (1953) to the legitimate drama to act in *Death Takes a Holiday*. Of his own part in the play he wrote, "I against my wishes, was cast in the part of Moses, in which I proved unsatisfactory." His participation was on surer ground in the dances and ballets which he created for the production—they were wholly successful.

He was not bitter on this score about his acting failure, for he had no acting ambitions or self-delusions. He was proud of his wife, and it was he who saved the glowing reviews heaped upon her. A long piece in the *Christian Science Monitor* reported, "Miss St. Denis proved herself an artist, an actress as interesting, perhaps, as any who have appeared on the classic stage of Berkeley's outdoor theater. She is gifted with a voice of unusual quality and a superbly responsive physique. The present writer, watching her, could not remember seeing half a dozen of the leading actresses of America or indeed of Europe who could surpass her in natural grace or individual appeal. Her performance was a revelation." Another critic spoke of a "brilliant and accomplished performance" and said that "students of acting had much to learn from Miss St. Denis."

Ted's adoration of St. Denis was unabated despite the tortures to which she actually, or in his mind, subjected him. It took tangible form in the two-volume book which he carefully researched, lovingly assembled, and glowingly wrote, *Ruth St. Denis: Pioneer and Prophet*, published in a limited (five hundred copies) signed edition in 1920. Volume One is text and includes a biography of St. Denis, synopses of her historic Oriental dances, press quotes, and commentaries and statements of vision. Volume Two provides exquisite reproductions of photographs of her (each individually mounted), most by such superlative photographers as Arnold Genthe. The initial price was fifty dollars the set; today, copies, when found, sell into the hundreds of dollars.

My own copy of *Pioneer and Prophet* came from Miss Ruth herself.

It was in 1938 when she headed the newly formed dance department at Adelphi College (now Adelphi University) in Garden City, New York. She was rummaging through some huge trunks in a storeroom. Newspapers clippings, photos, posters, books, bits of jewelry, a sari or two were jumbled together in that monumental disorder in which Miss Ruth thrived. A copy of *Pioneer and Prophet* turned up. "Ted must have given you this," she said. When I said no, she handed it to me very casually, "Take it, there must be more somewhere."

It is quite a wonderful book. It is designed in rather elaborate style for today's fashion, with beveled edges, illuminated lettering, miniature drawings such as one might find in books of fairy tales. The writing was fulsome yet somehow sincere, in tune with the rather flamboyant, adjectival style which was always to characterize Ted's writings, including his letters.

When St. Denis's acting performances and her poetry-dance tours kept her in California, she opened her own studio in Los Angeles, but this was a rehearsal studio and not a school—when Ted was touring, she occasionally taught at the Grand Street Shawn school if Martha was on the road. And the strange partnership also included a joint St. Denis-Shawn home in Los Angeles which they called Tedruth. It was here that Ted wrote *Pioneer and Prophet*, and it was here that they began to build the small but important dance library which contained not only books but photos, movies, and the earliest clippings of St. Denis which Ted had carefully assembled, sorted, dated, and pasted into scrapbooks. (Fifteen years later, when Ruth was writing her autobiography, *Ruth St. Denis: An Unfinished Life*, she ripped, snipped, and yanked items from the scrapbooks as she needed them and never replaced them. The jumbled trunks at Adelphi were the result. Ted never forgave her, but he should have expected it.)

Tedruth caught fire and burned down. The library was destroyed, and Ted spent years replacing the photos and clippings and redoing the scrapbooks. They moved to a nearby property which they called The Compound. Often Ruth was there alone. Of the burning of Tedruth, she wrote in her journal: "The fuse from a gas burner catches fire and burns a home. What is that to me? Perhaps a benefit in that I am obliged to tighten up the girdle of my spiritual loins and work harder to keep what is my birthright: love, beauty, life."

From Ted's military discharge in 1918 until the two reunited in 1922 for nearly a decade of performing and touring together, the period was described by the husband as "choppy." They were partly together, mostly apart, but it was to their advantage that they danced together on major occasions and both seemed to feel, despite their battles, that they had some need for each other on a personal level. But it was vacillation all the way.

Ted has described his week's confrontation with St. Denis in Detroit following his release from the army. St. Denis, in her journals and autobiography, also reports on the event. Both told me of this and the many subsequent rifts. Curiously, they agree pretty much on the bald facts, but their explanations, interpretations, and colorings are so different that I find myself shifting the blame back and forth as I read, or as I listened, to first one and then the other.

Ted saw Detroit as his heartbreak, not hers; an emotional statement of her ego needs, not his. He spoke of her accusations about his turning her into a robot and stifling her soul and her art. She reported his arrival in Detroit: "He woke me out of sleep with his dear, eager face bending over to tell me he was free." In her version he traveled with her for several weeks while they talked matters out. In these talks and in the exchange of letters, she admitted that she could be accused of being temperamental and unreasonable, that she had gone into the ideas of school and company in full accord with Ted's plans, and that now she wanted to withdraw. She was quite disarming about it. She admitted that her outbursts were "out of order" and that they caused her husband and others connected with the complex enterprise of company and school "endless anxieties and bewilderments. To them I was selfish and unreasonable . . . but stronger than their amazement was my own sense of destiny." She seemed to believe in the significance of Denishawn and of her husband's potential stature in American dance, but she was convinced that the creative work she had done in harness with him was of a lesser quality than she had accomplished before their union.

For them as husband and wife the situation was just as desperate. Ted found himself in "emotional agony most of the time. I was constantly being whipped—little sharp ends of something metallic would come—and whenever I felt that I was about to be relieved of

these hurts, others would be inflicted." Ruth felt that ultimate separation was inevitable, "in spite of our love for each other," because of
"artists' egotisms and our emotional dissonances."

On the artistic side she not only suggested that her own creative
standards were less when she worked with him, but she also shifted
the blame, justifiably or not, with the comment: "Ted was growing
restless of being forever coupled with me, both in performance and
in the mind of the world, and the constant preference of the public
and the critics for my work was creating a limiting and unjust attitude toward Ted's artistic growth." These words were written after
the final separation, but they were in her mind during the 1918 to
1922 period and much of the time thereafter. She never let anyone,
nor him, forget that she was the more important, the more gifted of
the two. She never protested at length about her superiority, except
in her bitchiest moments, for she was convinced of her own genius
and quite secure in it. But this very attitude sowed in Ted the self-
doubts which tormented him all his life. Intellectually he might have
fought her on her claims of superior talent, but she did not argue,
she assumed that she was a genius and assumed that everyone agreed
with her—most did.

On the home front she was equally disarming. She admitted all of
her peccadilloes. She even told him about other relationships in
those letters which wrenched his heart and attacked his spirit. So
again, he could not argue with a woman who said, "I have never
achieved a reconciliation between my life as an individual artist and
my heart as a woman. In this fact lay the seeds of my personal sor-
row." She was born with a passionate nature, she hurled herself at a
new love and faced insurmountable hurdles which, whenever possible, she skirted. At a given moment she didn't care what happened.
Later she might feel remorse, but during an affair, she cared not a
whit about her husband or her responsibilities. She kept him posted.

Subsequently he came to realize that most and perhaps all of these
affairs were romantic rather than erotic. One was a park ranger that
he later described as being "butch"; one was a teenager of whom he
said, "If he were any younger he'd be a foetus!"; another eventually
became the mayor of a fairly large western city. Many years later
Shawn and the mayor met and, on a man-to-man basis, the politician

confessed, "I went up into the hills with her and, frankly, I had screwing in mind but all she wanted to do was to read poetry to me by moonlight."

This, apparently, was no isolated event. Many years later, when she was a very old lady, Miss Ruth asked me why a certain publication was always so generous in reporting her by then less-than-startling activities. I asked a staff member who informed me that an executive in the publication had once spent a night with Ruth St. Denis on a hill in California and had never fully recovered from the romance of the occasion. I told Miss Ruth, but she had forgotten all about it. However, one night in the theater I saw him approaching us down the aisle, and I murmured to her the name of the publication and added, "night in moonlight California." As he leaned across me to speak to her, she looked up with radiant surprise and, in her caressive voice, said, "It has been so long . . ." He was a goner for another quarter of a century.

But for Ted Shawn, from the rude awakening in Detroit until the joint careers resumed in 1922 and sporadically thereafter, "It was hell, pure, unadulterated ghastly suffering such as I had never known."

He didn't dwell on her behavior, or misbehavior. Certainly, after their separation in 1930, he found himself free as an artist to stand on his own, and he loved it, and as far as his personal life was concerned, he was happier than he had ever been while married to a demanding, inconstant, unpredictable woman. Still, he never forgave her for her treatment of him. The male in him resented her deeply, the professional performer never wanted to see his association with her, a glamorous and historic one, dissolved. In later years his reaction to her name or to a letter from her or a story about her depended entirely upon his mood. It was just as easy for him to be the devoted, loving husband celebrating a continuing romance which was continuing only if it suited his purposes as it was to be the angry, deeply hurt, scarred mate. And he was, in my opinion, emotionally (or egoistically, at any rate) scarred.

9

Ted Shawn, as a dancer, choreographer and producer, had been building his reputation without St. Denis. In 1921, he rented New York's vast Metropolitan Opera House for a performance, an event which would culminate a national tour starring himself. Because of booking commitments he forfeited the time, but a few years later he was to give an enormously successful solo recital at the equally prestigious Carnegie Hall. The autumn 1921 tour, however, was a smashing success. A twenty-city tour, starting in Los Angeles, peaked at a matinee at New York's Apollo Theater, and it was there that one of the nation's foremost impresario-bookers, Daniel Mayer, saw him and determined to engage him and his dancers for a long-term contract. This association was to lead Ruth St. Denis and Ted Shawn to the popularity apex of their careers and to make Denishawn the most successful dance company in American history. Shawn told me that Mayer wanted him and his dancers and that it was he, Ted, who suggested that St. Denis be approached for a renewal of the partnership on a long-term contract basis. St. Denis told me that Mayer wanted her and that he urged Ted to use his influence to get her to agree. Whatever the sequence St. Denis agreed to a joint appearance with Shawn in Greensburg, Pennsylvania, in February of 1922 and to a conference with Mayer, at which point she signed a three-year contract.

Shawn's preceding transcontinental tour in which his assisting dancers were Martha Graham, Charles Weidman, Betty May, and Dorothea Bowen, with Horst as musical director, carried two programs. Program one was divided into six sections, and it is interesting to see the range of dance which Shawn offered and to note that he shrewdly combined dances which were of special interest to him and which he considered of high artistic merit along with numbers he was certain would divert, amuse, or excite audiences. This pattern he pursued throughout his long career—years later, audiences would sit through his attenuated religious solo, *The Hound of Heaven*, because the program promised his most popular solo, the American Indian *Invocation to the Thunderbird* and his sexy flamenco dances . . . if they were patient.

In 1921 Program one opened with *A Church Service in Dance*, modeled after a typical Protestant service and derived from that entire church service in dance he had performed so successfully in 1917 in San Francisco. He maintained that his pioneer efforts in Christian dance presentations led to St. Denis's explorations of religious dance and the founding of her Rhythmic Choir in later years when she was concerned primarily with dance and religion. His wife, however, explained it differently: "Stimulated by my long vision of the dance as the great instrument of worship, he had worked for several years on this conception."

Again, it is hard to say now who was right. Both perhaps.

Following the church ballet there was a suite of "music visualizations." These included the Shawn solo *Gnossienne*, the dance inspired by ancient Cretan bas-reliefs, set to music of Satie; an Afro-American *Juba* for the three girls; and dances to music of Chopin, Ferrari, Scarlatti, and a contemporary composer St. Denis had discovered first as an accompanist, Ilgenfritz. Third came a romantic suite which included a long popular St. Denis-Shawn duet, *Valse Directoire*, and the popular solo for Weidman, *Pierrot Forlorn*. Next was a Spanish dance section featuring Shawn and Graham in their successful *Malagueña* (to Moszkowski music and not to the later *Malagueña* of enormous popularity by Lecuona which Shawn danced as a solo in the 1930s). Fifth was the oddly titled *Oriental and Barbaric Suite*, in which Martha's *Orientale* most certainly was Oriental and Ted's *Invocation to the Thunderbird* (to music of Sousa), barbaric. This part also contained *Serenata Morisca*, the first solo Martha had been permitted to dance, and a solo which was to become a Shawn classic, *Japanese Spear Dance*. Java, Siam, and New Zealand (à la Maori) were also represented. Program one closed with an abridged version of *Xochitl* with Martha and Ted.

Program two contained a good many of the same dances but with some alternates of importance. Ted included a solo for himself, *Spring, Beautiful Spring*, also called *Frohsinn*, to saccharine music of Lincke, a sort of free-style ballet burst done in bare feet but with lots of ballet-rooted steps (audiences at home and abroad came to adore it); Martha and Charles did an Arab duet, and Martha and Ted did a duet from the old *Egyptian Ballet*.

Along with his Apollo success Shawn immediately opened a Denishawn School in New York. St. Denis was running Los Angeles Denishawn on Ted's behalf during the tour but left it in charge of a faculty and administrator in order to do the single duo program with Ted in February and to sign the historic contract. Her reasons for signing were as capricious as her general behavior, but it was no small help that Mayer charmed her (both Ted and Ruth report this to be true). "Why, after all my rebellions and resentments against the school and joint performances," she wrote, "I leaped to the idea of a long-term contract under Mayer is difficult to analyze. It may well be that I can never accomplish anything by myself, and that I intuitively knew this. Perhaps I must be mated to a running partner, visible or invisible, who believes in me and my vision. Otherwise, in the light of retrospection, I appear to wander about rather futilely, giving out little spurts of ideas, but never really settling down to a purpose." Mother St. Denis and Buzz (Brother) had been her running mates for the great *Radha*, *Egypta*, *O-Mika* productions, and Ted had held her in harness briefly. She knew she had been frittering, and distasteful as it was, she was aware that her future needed Ted's organizational strength, along with his continuing devotion, and Mayer's prestige. The latter won her to a contract in two ways: (1) "An instantaneous affection sprang up between us that weathered business difficulties and temperamental disagreements," and (2) "Through him, for the first time in years, we would have money on a large scale, and be able to create the ballets we longed to do." To her journals she confided that the arrangement by no means solved either her creative or spiritual needs, but that it was pertinent for a given period.

She returned to California to teach at Denishawn. Ted taught at Eastern Denishawn and in April 1922, Ruth St. Denis, Ted Shawn, and their Denishawn Dancers were reborn with a tour of the South, followed by vaudeville performances in London and, beginning in

October 1922, the first of three Daniel Mayer-booked national tours which would take them into well over one hundred cities! The two subsequent tours, concluding in the spring of 1925, were also exhaustively booked.

The preview tour of the South and the London engagement were, of course, arranged by Mayer to break in the company and to get reviews. The core of the troupe was basically Ted's, augmented by other dancers. The repertory was pretty much the same except that now the St. Denis solos were added and some St. Denis-Shawn duets revived. The big, new, lavish productions were to come later.

The London season was theatrically successful if not a happy experience on the personal level. St. Denis was hesitant to return to England, believing that in the fourteen years she had been gone, she had nothing of artistic progress to show them. She fretted about this, blamed Ted for having held her back, but once again won English hearts with her dancing. Ted was miserable because his wife was blaming him for her lack of important new St. Denis creations and because she was hammering at him to remember his post as her servitor. Also, she had fallen in love again (Ted described it as "Ruth was searching for romance in all directions but me"). Martha was miserable because St. Denis had taken *Xochitl* from her (although St. Denis freely admitted she was not Martha's equal in the fiery role) and because Louis Horst's wife, Betty, was along on the trip, and Martha was deeply in love with Louis. This, then, was the brief period when Ted and Martha discovered that misery loves company and, therefore, kept company.

There were nonperformance events that were to have a major impact on Ted. They had, of course, the lively social side, being wined, dined, and lionized by celebrities; Ruth returned to pay homage again to her earthly trinity of Westminster Abbey (St. Faith's Chapel), the Egyptian exhibit at the British Museum, and the Elgin Marbles; Ted was seeing England for the very first time and, after going to his first English tailor, bedazzled even his wife in a cutaway, gray waistcoat, silk hat, gloves, and walking stick—what she described as "a truly breathtaking picture." But the real event was a visit with the great psychologist-philosopher Havelock Ellis, whose major work, *Studies in the Psychology of Sex*, was then a shocking milestone in man's progress in understanding his own behavior. St.

Denis, of course, had always referred to Ellis as the patron saint of the dance, principally because of his essay, "The Dance of Life."

Both Ruth and Ted visited him together and in separate sessions. It was Ted's first opportunity to talk with a true philosopher, with a mature man who was both a scientist and a lover of the arts. For the first time he was able to hear someone discuss sex easily and homosexuality without embarrassment. Perhaps he found out that homosexuality, in the twentieth century, was not abnormal and should not, in the light of man's behavior and sexual necessities, be considered a sin, even though it was viewed as a crime. It is likely that his readings of ancient Greek culture and the acceptance of male-for-male love were removed from myth and placed into reality for him by Ellis. To both St. Denis and Shawn he gave a letter of introduction to Edward Carpenter, who had written eloquently of yoga and of love and desire and fulfillment. Barriers of custom, bigotries, insensibilities were pushed aside by this gentle, passionate man. Carpenter was past eighty when he received a note from the two American dancers, yet he left his country home and journeyed to London to see them dance, to talk with them and to give Ted, especially, a new insight into the totality of love, of love without Puritan or Victorian taboos.

Carpenter, Shawn told me, was homosexual, or bisexual, and because he was a gentleman and a sage as well as an accomplished writer, the stereotype of the homosexual implanted in young Ted by tradition was erased. At the time he had not had homosexual experiences, or so he said, but he knew what was latent within him, and the talks with Ellis and Carpenter were important to him then and of essential support to him when he turned to men for love.

After six weeks in England (the Coliseum in London, Bristol, Manchester), they returned to America for a summer session at an arts center, Mariarden, at Peterboro, New Hampshire. Distinguished artists were engaged to train the young in the theater. Theresa Helburn, later a cofounder of the Theatre Guild; Margaret Anglin and Edith Wynne Matheson, actresses; Kenneth MacGowan, producer-director; Tony Sarg, the marionettist; Richard Bennett and Adrienne Morrison, great stars of the theater, were among them. Ted and Ruth were to teach dance to children and young girls. Two

of the pupils were Francesca and Berthe Braggiotti of that remarkably talented Florentine family of musical parents and four boys and
four girls who had moved to Boston and brought their multiple talents with them. Francesca and Berthe studied the Denishawn system
avidly at Mariarden, and when the summer was over, opened a
Denishawn branch (the first of several such schools) in Brookline,
Massachusetts.

Francesca went on to become a successful dancer, a featured
player in an Italian movie and, ultimately, the wife of John Davis
Lodge, actor turned politician (later governor of Connecticut and
ambassador to Spain, etc.). Ted became a close friend of the
Braggiottis and told me of family conclaves when all ten of them
sang, danced, and played a variety of musical instruments. Berthe
died very young and Ted said that in death, she was put into her
dancing dress, seated in a chair, and that the family performed so
that Berthe would leave them with the joy and beauty she had
shared with them. Ted, and later Miriam Winslow, one of his most
gifted pupils and a participant in the Braggiotti Denishawn School
before she went on to make her own name in the dance world, fed
me stories of the talented and, apparently, very beautiful Braggiottis.
Once, when I was lecturing at the Philadelphia Art Alliance, I noticed a ravishingly beautiful woman in the audience. It was almost
impossible for me to take my eyes off her. At the end of the lecture I
was delighted to see that she had come backstage along with some
others. "Let me introduce myself," she said. I halted her and
blurted, "You must be a Braggiótti," although I had never seen her
or a picture of her before. "I am," she laughed. "I'm Gloria."

There were, of course, performances as well as teaching duties at
Mariarden. In London Ted had shocked many of the English with
the scantiness of his costumes; at Mariarden he had the cook in a
state of outrage when she heard he planned—and a man at that!—to
perform nude. The story swept through the servants' quarters and
into the village, and the Guy Curriers, who ran Mariarden, were
worried about a possible scandal. Ted screamed that a cook should
not be a censor. Ruth, agreeing with him, suggested an invited audience instead of an open-to-the-public affair.

For the program, St. Denis presented, in the outdoor theater in
the moonlight, some of the girls in a hieratic, friezelike Egyptian

dance. They had little on, but it was a cool, formal ritual in the softness of moonlight. No one objected. And then the scene turned to a figure of the Greek god Adonis on a pedestal. He seemed to be of marble, and he wore only the conventional fig leaf. The audience applauded the pure beauty of the statuary. Then it moved, and Ted Shawn, in a series of thirty-two poses, gave the première of his *The Death of Adonis* plastique to a cheering audience, perhaps even including the cook. (In fact the performance almost did not take place, but not for reasons of censorship. In an earlier performance Ted had done a Greek dance, and the fresh wreaths supplied him by eager, helpful students were made of beautifully garlanded poison ivy.)

The three Mayer tours, though placing a tremendous burden upon the dancers—each tour ran from October until May—were richly rewarding. Vaudeville appearances had taken them into big cities where they had become favorites with the vaudeville-going public. The concert tours took them not only to cities but to towns and villages, and by playing literally hundreds of cities their names became household words: Denishawn was a familiar trademark, dance and Denishawn were almost synonymous, and Ruth St. Denis and Ted Shawn were, in a very real sense, the superstars of their day. The money they earned—and it was plenty—enabled them to mount lavish productions, much bigger than Ted had been able to do with his vaudeville ballets, splendid as those were.

In the Denishawn era the impact of the "live" show should not be underestimated. There was no radio entertainment until the mid-1920s, and certainly no television during the great years of Ruth St. Denis and Ted Shawn—1915 to 1930—as mass media for entertainment. In fact it was impossible to experience professional entertainment in the home. One had to go out. The mass medium of entertainment was, of course, the movies, but with most movies went vaudeville and on almost every vaudeville circuit in the country one could find a Denishawn act.

By their exhaustive tours Ruth St. Denis and Ted Shawn with their Denishawn productions came closer to saturating the land with their brand of art-entertainment than any other single act. There were stock companies appearing in plays, and dramatic stars took to the road, but the names of the plays changed and stars changed. A constant on the scene, on billboards, on both concert and vaudeville programs, were the continuing names: St. Denis, Shawn, Deni-shawn.

As a child in my hometown I remember hearing the name Deni-shawn. Someone was asking about a little girl I knew and my mother said, "Oh, she's taking classes at Denishawn." I didn't know what Denishawn meant at the time, but I can still recall my mother's voice and the way she pronounced "Denishawn"—she made it sound very important. It was, in my hometown and in everyone's hometown. The branches of the Denishawn school attracted pupils, and they at-tracted pupils because the kids and their parents (or mothers, at least) had seen Ruth St. Denis, Ted Shawn, and their fabulous dance shows.

Ted chided Ruth for the enormous production expenses of her Babylonian ballet, *Ishtar*, whose sets weighed several tons; but she countered that his comparable ballet was *Feather of the Dawn*, which reproduced an entire Indian pueblo on stage! I remember Ted moan-ing to me about his wife's extravagances as he reminisced about the great Mayer days. "*Ishtar*," he said, "not only had seven gates but every goddamn gate opened and shut on hinges!" Indeed, the first production, premiered in Atlantic City, was so unwieldy that it sim-ply could not go on tour, and a lighter, but still elaborate, *Ishtar* toured the nation.

Of course Denishawn played New York, Chicago, Boston, San Francisco, Pittsburgh, Denver, Charleston, and Atlanta, but the company also danced in Shamokin, Elyria, Kalamazoo, Sandusky, Coffeyville, Keokuk, Manitowoc, Beaver Falls, and you name it. Sometimes the dancers were not even quite sure themselves where they were. They traveled by train, and it was the job of the com-pany manager to follow the route list and get them to the right place at the right time. Trains, taxis, hotels, theaters in whatever order were his problems. Ted tells of the morning that he and Ruth hopped out of a hotel bed and decided to go shopping. They left the hotel and started down the street of an average American city. "What town is this?" asked Ruth. "I don't know," replied Ted, "but I have the route list in my pocket so we'll just check there. What's the date?" "I don't know." So they had to go up to a policeman and ask, "Where are we?" Ted reported that the officer looked at them to see if they could possibly be vagrants. "I think he settled for dual amnesia," suggested St. Denis.

For the first tour—1922 to 1923—the program was composed of music visualizations, various *divertissements,* and an Oriental section. St. Denis, in the visualizations, included a solo which had started as an improvisation at a party and remained to become one of her most famous dances, *Waltz and Liebestraum* (Brahms and Liszt). Denishawn legend had it that it was St. Denis's love song in dance to her husband, and it became something of a tradition that as she finished it and exited into the wings with her head thrown back, her white hair falling loosely and her arms outstretched, that Ted picked her up and carried her to her dressing room. He told me, however, that it had been created for some callow youth during one of her romantic escapades, and she told me that on one occasion when they had had a particularly bad tiff, she had added *Liebestraum* to her dances as a gesture of "forgive me," but that as she approached him where he was standing in the wings, he turned his back on her, walked to his dressing room, and slammed the door.

The *divertissement* section included a St. Denis-Shawn duet, the *Malagueña,* which he had often danced with Martha; *Tango* for himself; and a St. Denis solo which played under several titles, the most common being *Spanish Shawl Plastique.* St. Denis herself was the first to admit that her Spanish dance footwork left much to be desired. Once she said to me, "Ted was a brilliant Spanish dancer but I got as far as accomplishing a *zapateado uno* and threw in the towel! Teddy gave me something to do with a shawl, and that was much better."

One of the most important St. Denis dance heresies in 1906 was that she was a dancer without concern for routine steps. A Boston critic shortly thereafter pointed out, while praising her to the skies, that she was not noted for "elaborate foot work" and that she was primarily "a gestural dancer." In her autobiography she herself reports that when she was five, her father handed her a tambourine and, "I started beating out the time, with some uncertain footwork to accompany it, a line of conduct I have followed ever since."

In subsequent programs, mainly because of Shawn's Spanish dance skills, Spanish sections were enlarged even to the inclusion of a full-scale—soloists and company—*cuadro flamenco*. But for the first tour, *Egyptian Ballet* and *Xochitl* (with Martha) were the big productions.

The second Mayer tour—1923 to 1924—included two major innovations in the music visualizations. Ted did an all-male (five dancers, himself included) work to the MacDowell *Polonaise* (years later this went into the repertory of the Men Dancers), and St. Denis and Doris Humphrey collaborated (it was Humphrey's choreography with St. Denis's supervision and direction) on *Sonata Tragica* to music of MacDowell. Part way through the tour St. Denis suggested to Doris that the music be dropped and that the work be danced in silence. It became, as far as anyone knows, the first unaccompanied dance in the history of the American theater. Years later Miss Ruth said to me, "I never danced in it but I used to watch it at most performances and I suddenly realized that the music was not needed. Doris's choreographic form was so clear, so perfect, so total. I remember saying to her, 'Dear, you make your own music in *Tragica*, so let's try it without MacDowell.' It worked."

There was also, as a major number, an adapted version of St. Denis's great solo, *The Spirit of the Sea*, which she had first performed in 1915, now done with Shawn and company. I asked her once what the differences were between the two versions. "Not much, dear. I was still the sea. Teddy was a fisherman. Somewhere along the line I drowned him. It was still *my* dance."

The Oriental, the exotic, the semiethnic were always present— *Balinese Fantasy* (created two years before they ever saw Bali), *Vision of the Aissoua, Siamese Ballet* (years before they had seen Siam), Miss Ruth's Chinese *Kuan Yin,* and her Hindu *Dance of the Black and Gold Sari*—but Ted's concern with Americana was by no means neglected. Programs included *Five American Sketches* which contained the *Crapshooter* solo for Charles, Ted's famous *Invocation to the Thunderbird, Around the Hall, Gringo Tango, Boston Fancy—1854.* Miss Ruth also included her much admired *The Peacock* and her portrait of *Theodora* (the ex-circus dancer who became Empress of Byzantium).

The production numbers were, of course, elaborate but the origins of some of the costumes for the Oriental extravaganzas were Main Street America. Ted told me of the time on tour when he and Ruth, with shopping time, went into a Woolworth's, headed for the kitch-

enware aisle and began putting sieves, colanders, and funnels on
their heads, shouting across counters to each other: "Look, dear, this
strainer fits perfectly." The clerks, understandably, recoiled from
this mad couple. They never knew that in a few weeks, with gold
and silver paint added, Woolworth "jewels" glued on, and a funnel
secured to an inverted sieve, that a dazzling Siamese headdress
would emerge.

At the close of the first Mayer tour in 1923 Martha left the company to go into the *Greenwich Village Follies*, produced by Shawn's
long-time producer friend, John Murray Anderson. Ted always said
that Martha left because of the complications over Louis and Betty
Horst. Martha says she left because the time had come for her to
find her own way in dance, and the *Follies* was a steppingstone to
that independence which would revolutionize dance not only in
America but in the world. Her first numbers during her two years
with Anderson were either Denishawn dances or new ones cast in
the Denishawn mold. Her post-*Follies* teaching duties at the East-
man School of Music in Rochester were mainly exploratory, and her
first New York concert in 1926 listed many numbers which, if they
were not Denishawn, owed much to that period. It was not until
1927 that she gave a recital that shook the dance and theater worlds
with its total rebellion against all things Denishawn, with its starkness of dress (Martha herself later called it her "period of long
woolens"), its angularity of movement, its masklike face, its disturb-
ing themes.

Within Denishawn many of Martha's roles were inherited by her
younger sister Georgia "Jeordie" Graham. Jeordie (the "Georgia"
was permanently replaced by "Jeordie" in 1925) resembled Martha
but she was a far gentler person—Martha had been the tempestuous
boss of make-believe playtime in the childhood of the Graham sisters
Martha, Mary, and Jeordie—and a less explosive dancer.

Shawn told me that once on a tour train Miss Ruth got up and
walked over to Jeordie and for no apparent reason said, "Dear, you
are never going to make it. Why do you try?" and walked off. Ted
said, "If you had told Ruth later what she had done, that she had destroyed a not very secure ego, she would have denied it, and she
would have been truthful because she would have forgotten all about
it. Ruth always said what popped into her head. It popped right out,

and she never remembered whether she had amused or destroyed someone."

Just as the Denishawners had been the first dancers to perform at the Greek Theater in Berkeley on the West Coast in 1916 in a triumphant invasion of a great outdoor theater dedicated to serious drama, so they became, in 1925, the first to invade the East Coast's outdoor temple of music, Lewisohn Stadium in uptown New York City. At each of their five Lewisohn seasons (the last was in 1931), they presented programs which stressed repertory favorites, but new pieces, especially designed for the Stadium, were also produced. In 1925 the premiere was *Straussiana,* a Johann Strauss opus with Shawn as a dashing hussar and St. Denis as a glamorous lady of Vienna. (A short movie segment, showing an excerpt from this and the thousands who jammed the Stadium, still exists.)

Whether or not the Denishawners hold the attendance record for Stadium events depends on one's view of the facilities, for seating areas were extended after the Denishawn era to accommodate vaster audiences. Certainly, for the capacity of the Stadium at that time, the Denishawners were the undisputed stars. At one performance, by late afternoon, there were lines of people along the four city blocks which bounded the Stadium waiting to get in for the evening performance.

The first spectacle to be done expressly for the Stadium was St. Denis's *The Lamp* (1928), which required almost fifty dancers. It was her first mystical ballet on a large scale. There are two delicious stories about it. One was told to me by Martha Bigelow Eliot, a Boston dancer who worked occasionally with Denishawn. Martha was a young matron with children, and for one of the rehearsals of *The Lamp* she was just an understudy. Miss Ruth, who never could remember names, summoned her at one point by calling out, "Where is the girl who is always in a family way?" Martha responded and was told to clamber to the top of a mountain which Miss Ruth had caused to be constructed on the stage. At the peak was a glass floor through which shone the lights which St. Denis wished to suffuse her body. To check the effect Martha had been sent to the pinnacle. While standing there the glass gave way and Martha tumbled (unhurt) down the mountain and rolled to the edge of the stage. "Wonderful, dear," shouted Miss Ruth. "We'll keep it." And the story goes that in performance, St. Denis hurled herself off her mountain to spectacular effect.

Ted told of a performance of *The Lamp* when St. Denis, as usual, was perturbed about a lighting effect. The stage was covered with her draperies, and minions were placed under it to make them billow. The light was pink, a color the lighting-conscious St. Denis never used in mystical moments. "Where's Anna?" she hissed. A voice at her feet under the drapes replied, "We've sent for her, Miss Ruth." A rivulet worked its way across the stage and beached at Miss Ruth's feet. "Anna," said the star, "that idiot is using a pink 'gel'; I want a blue." The rivulet receded all the way to the wings. Soon the pink faded to blue and the rivulet eddied back to find out if all was well. "Won't do," murmured St. Denis. "Wrong shade."

Other Stadium firsts included Shawn's all-men (fourteen) music visualization to Honegger's *Pacific-231;* Shawn's *Jurgen,* based on the controversial James Branch Cabell novel of the same name, starring St. Denis and Shawn; St. Denis's *Angkor-Vat,* with St. Denis and a company of more than forty; St. Denis's *A Buddhist Festival* and *The Prophetess* (with more than fifty dancers); Shawn's *Job: A Masque for Dancing* (more than sixty dancers). And there were more. These Stadium dates marked the Denishawn debuts of many who were to go on to become famous in their own spheres. Paul Haakon, the young Danish dancer with a leap to match Nijinsky's, was one; another was Jack Cole, who was to become a major force in theatrical dance for night clubs, stage shows, movies; and another was Barton Mumaw, destined to play a major role in the life of Ted Shawn. Mumaw first danced for Denishawn in 1930.

The Stadium, which presided over so many large-scale Denishawn productions, also had an even more famous first in a simple duet, *Josephine and Hippolyte* (1928), which became one of the most popular pieces in the last years of Denishawn. It was a dashing, romantic piece with a heroine and a handsome Napoleonic officer. It had been inspired by a set of jewelry, once belonging to the Empress Josephine and given to her by Napoleon, which Shawn had purchased and presented to his wife. The huge Stadium public and audiences on tour sighed happily as they watched the dance world's most famous couple talking, whispering to each other as they smilingly, coquettishly danced to the syrupy music of Drigo. To the audience, they were the epitome of romance: they were making love. My own dance teacher, Phoebe Barr (at that time Phoebe Baughan), who performed in the last Denishawn engagements, put me straight. "Miss Ruth never could remember the steps and Mr. Shawn was always telling her where to go next." Shawn verified this to me: "She'd waltz by me and say, 'Teddy, what do I do next?' And I'd say, 'Ruthie, take six steps stage right, turn, look, hold out your arm and I'll come back to tell you what's after that.' She never learned it, but then she was apt to improvise everything anyhow."

Years later, when they had left their youth behind them, they revived this dance at Ted's Jacob's Pillow. At the dress rehearsal Ruth said, "Teddy, you may have to cue me occasionally, dear. You may never have noticed it in the old days, but I never did know it terribly well."

The Stadium years and the great national tours were interrupted by what may well have been the crowning experience of the whole Denishawn era, the 1925 to 1926 tour of the Orient, the first time that Ruth St. Denis, who had introduced the dance art of the East to America, had ever visited the source of her inspiration. It was the first time too, for Shawn, long attracted to Oriental philosophies Oriental lavishness of costume, Oriental faiths in gods who danced.

The three-year Daniel Mayer tours and the triumphant Stadium seasons had served to keep Ruth St. Denis and Ted Shawn together not simply as husband and wife but as the essential, in-harness leaders of the nation's major theatrical troupe. Furthermore the Denishawn schools, scattered around the nation, required their joint concern. The Boston Braggiotti Denishawn had been the first, and as other dance schools were franchised to use the name, St. Denis and Shawn were committed to an agreement whereby they not only approved the dance curricula in such schools but also agreed to teach in person a certain number of classes per year.

Denishawn had become a big business and the two cochairmen could not become disassociated from each other and their joint enterprises without destroying their lucrative, artistically and financially, commodity. But of all the functions of Denishawn, the one that kept them together was, of course, dancing together, performing together as they were committed by contract to do.

As Ted said, with eight shows a week and all their other commitments there was hardly time for his wife to get involved in any new romantic attachments at this time. It was work, performing, creating, teaching, success, money. It was all too good to jeopardize. There were bickerings, outright fights, screaming tantrums, but Ted's vision of the Greater Denishawn had come true. He held Ruth to it, and he disciplined himself to put up with her tirades about his turning her into a robot, stifling her and forcing her to worship his god, *success*.

The Oriental tour was booked by an impresario, Asway Strok, himself an Oriental who arranged with Daniel Mayer for the Denishawn tour. The Denishawners constituted the first American dance company to play the Far East. They took with them four programs, and they danced in Japan, China, India, Indonesia, the Philippines, Singapore, Burma, Ceylon, Malaya, Indochina, Hong Kong, and what is now Pakistan (then part of India).

Both St. Denis and Shawn were excited about the forthcoming tour. As they wound up their transcontinental engagements under Mayer, Miss Ruth told the company everything she knew about the arts and philosophies of Asia from the books she had read, from Orientals she had known, from her theosophist connections. Ted, always an avid reader, devoured everything about the Far East he could find, and he too instructed the dancers who would be making the trip. Here in America they had often devoted one third of a program to dances of the East, and St. Denis had won her American and European reputation as an Oriental dancer—one newspaper, in 1906, had headlined her as "A Jersey Hindoo."

Were they taking coals to Newcastle? They thought about it and worried about it. Shawn told me that for the most part they avoided doing their Japanese dances in Japan, their Indian dances in India and so on. Miss Ruth was terrified that her nonauthentic gestures to non-Indian music in her East Indian dances would be inviting disaster. To the contrary she was idolized, especially in her *Dance of the Black and Gold Sari*. This particular solo had come about by chance. At Denishawn school, St. Denis had been instructing the girls on how to take the yards of the East Indian woman's traditional dress, the sari, and fold it, secure it, cover their heads and limbs with it. Once she taught it while music was being played, and an onlooker said, "It's a dance!" It became one and something of a St. Denis trademark. A rani, seeing it in India, told St. Denis, "Ah, only a lady of quality knows how to put on a sari as you do." And Doris Humphrey told me, "When we played in India, it seemed to us that Miss Ruth had to encore *Black and Gold* so much that we used to say that we'd do a number, then Miss Ruth would do *Black and Gold*, then we'd do something else, then she'd be back to do it again. It really was the smash hit of the performances in India."

Wherever they went, they not only performed, they also studied with Oriental dance masters. Ted especially applied himself to mastering exact techniques in the lands he visited. He made voluminous notes, took silent movies of performances, snapped still photographs, collected costumes and sketches, and assembled the materials which would serve, for years to come, in Denishawn productions and in Denishawn classes. Miss Ruth took instruction too, but she, as always, was more deeply concerned with the philosophies and the religious backgrounds of the Eastern theater. She was as much inspired by the Altar of Heaven in Peking as she was by the elaborate court dances of Java. Both served her well. For in subsequent seasons, her simple and radiantly quiet *Buddhist Nun* became as popular as her rich and glittering *A Javanese Court Dancer*.

It was in India that Shawn created one of his most famous solos, *The Cosmic Dance of Shiva*. A dance such as this serves as a perfect example of Ted Shawn's wedding of meaning with theatricality. Not that the two are antithetical, but in Shawn's case he could almost always translate something which had been intellectually and spiritually stimulating to him into theatrical terms of such a flashy nature that even untutored audiences could enjoy at least the surface sheen of the act. Miss Ruth had a similar gift, of course. In her historic *Radha* of 1906 her East Indian sermon was that man should reject the ephemeral attractions of the senses for spiritual purity, but she made the senses so attractive that audiences went wild about the dances and probably ignored the moral, if they ever bothered to notice its presence at all.

Shiva contained much of the ancient symbolism connected with India's dancing god. Shawn received instruction in technique, in theology, in costuming. His dance was warmly approved by Indian connoisseurs. Yet later this very solo would prove to be a smash in, of all surroundings, the *Ziegfeld Follies!*

If the Orient provided the Denishawners with untold riches, they in their turn brought much to the Far East. Writers were quick to report that St. Denis, authentic or not in step and gesture, had, with her Oriental dances, captured the spirit of the dance of India, relished and celebrated that spirit as she performed and communicated the joy of it to those watching her. She left an indelible mark in India. Essays and even books were written about her, some in Sanskrit, the language of the holy books of Hinduism. It was also said by Indian artists and scholars that she was responsible to a great degree for the renascence of the dance as an art form in India.

During World War II while I was stationed in Egypt, I met an officer of Britain's Royal Air Force who was an Indian. He was a physician, but he told me that his high-caste family had always been dancers by avocation. I asked him if he knew of Martha Graham. No, he did not. I mentioned several American dance stars other than those made famous by movies. He had heard of none . . . except for Ruth St. Denis and La Meri. St. Denis, he told me his parents had informed him, had given India a new vision of its ancient dances, and he had read much about her in Indian books. The Texan La Meri (Russell Meriwether Hughes) had come to India as a dancer-scholar and had mastered the country's dances, especially the classical, elegant, and intricate *bharat natyam*, to perfection.

Ted's *Adonis* was as popular in the Orient as St. Denis's *Nautch* and the perennial *Black and Gold Sari*, and both of them, along with their dancers, brought enormous prestige to America.

In Japan a long and detailed account appearing in a major newspaper concluded, "Whenever a historian tries to write a book on the relations between the U.S. and Japan, he cannot ignore the coming of the Denishawn Dancers in 1925 to Japan, because by their appearance on the stage of Tokyo, the Japanese attitude toward America in respect to art has been completely changed. In other words the historian must pay more attention to Ruth St. Denis and Ted Shawn than to any other visitors since Admiral Perry."

The Japanese had noted American prominence in matters of science, technology, and finance and had supposed, until Denishawn visited them, that what art America bothered to support was imported. Miss Ruth, in her journals, noted that "the Japanese, quick to catch meanings, said that our visit had done more than all the tele-

phones and battleships to make a sympathetic understanding between two great peoples. They had not known until we came that
America also worshipped beauty."

Thirty years later, when Martha Graham and her company would
tour the Far East for our somewhat wiser Department of State, she
too would read in a hitherto anti-American publication in Indonesia
that Indonesians had assumed that America was the land of "the
gadget, the dollar, and the bomb," until Graham had arrived to
show them that "America has a soul."

Once again Ruth St. Denis and Ted Shawn had made history,
had pioneered, had shown the way. Even though St. Denis was certainly the more idolized of the two, it is equally certain that the Oriental tour would never have taken place without Shawn, for even if
his wife remained the superstar of the duo, it was he who had made
the contract with Mayer which led them to the peak of their profession in America, he who made arrangements with Strok and in both
cases wheedled St. Denis into participating. Without her the great
American tours and the fabulous Oriental tour would probably
never have taken place. Without him they wouldn't have taken place
either.

It was the peak of Denishawn. But St. Denis even then sensed the
slow dissolution of the great experiment and experience. Martha had
left and with her went one of the most unique of Denishawn products. Although both Humphrey and Weidman were invaluable, their
own defection was not far off. Louis Horst, in 1925, followed
Martha's lead and left for studies in Germany and ultimate association with Martha in a long relationship which would forever influence Graham. Denishawn, musically, had relied heavily on Louis.
They had fine musical directors later, among them Clifford
Vaughan, who did the Oriental tour and subsequent engagements.
He too composed, as did Horst, as well as conducted and gave the
Denishawners expert musical help, but there was never another
Louis, gruff, hardworking, enormously gifted. Miss Ruth saw the
end dimly in the future.

She also saw increasing troubles in her married life. Even in the
midst of the great Oriental experience, she rebelled against the very
nature of the journey. She wished she could have been alone. She
wished that she had not been saddled with performances and sched-

ules. She wished that Ted would not strangle her need for independence. She wrote in her journal: "Underneath these exciting days is running the thread of Ted's and my personal life. Hours of continued deep companionship, other hours of dissonance. Very terrible and very real is the fact that to the one I love best I bring unrest and insecurity and pain, when I would bring joy and help and peace. What is my place—my being? Is marriage a right state for me? I honestly do not know what is right to do."

As their ship neared San Francisco's Golden Gate, she wrote a final line, "The great waves are dashing against the black rock." The voyage for Ruth St. Denis and Ted Shawn was also nearing its close. It was almost 1927. Three years later, they would tour together for the last time as heads of Denishawn, and shortly thereafter Denishawn would cease to exist. Their personal lives would be dashed to pieces by self-needs, self-doubts, weariness of each other, and new and tormenting loves.

10

During the long engagements of the Oriental tour, Ruth had time to experience new romances, which she hastened to tell Ted about, but both of them have recorded that much of the eighteen-month period was congenial, especially on the talk level. They had met, wooed, and wed in the midst of endless conversations on art and esthetics, and with the stimuli of their new discoveries in the Far East their conversations were extended.

Immediately on their return the Denishawners set out on perhaps the most triumphant tour they would ever experience. They had arrived in late November and on December 6, they opened in Los Angeles. Four months later, they wound up with matinee and evening performances at New York's Carnegie Hall. They returned with new numbers, fabulous costumes, new ideas, and, of course, new prestige from the Orient. Miss Ruth had created her solo, *White Jade*, inspired by the Altar of Heaven in Peking ("Here a vision of white jade as the supreme symbol of Chinese beauty came to me."), a quiet, almost motionless dance (except for a few slow steps and gestures), which was to become, because of its almost haloed beauty, an audience favorite. Ted had mastered the art of makeup and the art of swift costume change (although St. Denis had used this before in her Japanese dance drama *O-Mika* in 1913) in his Japanese *Momijii Gari*, in which he played both the heroine and the demon.

One entire section of this tour was called "Gleanings from Buddha-Fields." It began with St. Denis performing an invocation to Buddha and went on to visit Japan with *Momijii Gari*; China, with *White Jade* and *General Wu's Farewell to His Wife*; Java, with *A Javanese Court Dancer* and *Impressions of the Wayang Purwa*; Burma, with *Yein Pwe*; and India, with *The Soul of India* (a St. Denis solo),

123

Shawn's *The Cosmic Dance of Shiva* and *In the Bunnia Bazaar*. Oriental dividends included *Singhalese Devil Dance*, for three men (Ceylon); Miss Ruth's old favorite, *Japanese Flower Arrangement* and *Kuan Yin* (the Chinese Goddess of Mercy—and in Japan she added its Japanese counterpart, *Kwannon*); *Danse Cambodienne* (a solo for Jeordie Graham). Old favorites—the Toltecan *Xochitl*, the Babylonian *Ishtar*, and the Spanish suites, including *Cuadro Flamenco*, were also included, along with music visualizations, Americana, and *divertissements* on the four bills they carried with them.

The concluding performances—four of them—were epoch-making. No nonsymphonic artists had ever played four consecutive performances at prestigious Carnegie to capacity houses. Certainly no American dancers had ever drawn such crowds. Eastern Denishawn, as a school, was also located in Carnegie Hall's maze of studios, and it was bursting at the seams. It was a grand finale. But somehow those glittering performances in April of 1927 seemed like a beginning, as if an historic, glamorous past could have nothing but an even more glorious future. The tour, booked by a major impresario, Arthur Judson, had been an unparalleled success, and the culminating Carnegies had not only lifted the Denishawners to new peaks of prominence but had also elevated American dance to a position where it could not be ignored.

These performances and the prestige of Denishawn led directly to the engaging of two dance critics for New York's two major morning newspapers, the *New York Times* and the *New York Herald Tribune*. Carl Van Vechten and Mary Fanton Roberts had been among the distinguished and knowledgeable writers on dancing whose critiques and essays had appeared from time to time in newspapers, but newspapers themselves had no staff dance critics. The few there were wrote for the old *The Dance Magazine* or for *Denishawn Magazine*, published briefly by Denishawn in the mid-1920s.

It was Ted Shawn who pointed out to editors that even fifth-rate musicians were given the courtesy of reviews by trained music critics but that dancers were granted no such courtesies. Music critics, ill-equipped to review dance, were assigned the job of covering the dance recitals that came along. Why music critics and not drama critics? My own personal theory—and Shawn later said he believed I had guessed right—was that serious dancers referred to their performances as concerts. Sometimes recitals. To a city editor, the word "concert" was enough and off went the man that covered concerts, the music critic. Dancers then and now dislike being reviewed by music critics. Most would prefer drama critics in the absence of dance critics, since they feel themselves to be theater.

Martha Graham once remarked that if she could not be reviewed by a dance critic, she would prefer a sports writer. "Music critics listen to me dance," she said, "and that's wrong. At least a sports writer starts with the body. The body is what I start with."

The first full-time newspaper dance critic was Mary Watkins for the *New York Herald Tribune*. She was followed not many weeks later by John Martin, who was to become America's most famous and influential dance critic, on the *New York Times*. It was 1927. After a few years, Miss Watkins, wife of the music critic Edward Cushing, retired to have a family and the *Herald Tribune* made do with music critics again until I came to the *Trib* in the fall of 1939.

Martin, a man of theater, became interested in the new dance developments, modern dance, beginning with Martha Graham, who gave her first truly controversial program in New York in 1927, then with the maverick Helen Tamiris, and subsequently with Humphrey and Weidman, who defected from Denishawn in 1928. Watkins tried to steer a course that would be fair to the Denishawn era in its twilight days, fair to what little ballet there was in America, and fair to the rebellious, innovative, experimental moderns. Martin, on the other hand, took up the as yet unpopular cause of the modern dancers and with the power of the *Times* behind him, fostered the new form, brought it constantly to the attention of the public, educated and cajoled and demanded that people accept the new form. There are many who feel that without John Martin the great modern dance movement in America would have died a-borning with survival possible only for the superpioneers like Graham.

Soon after his appointment it was necessary for John Martin to review a Denishawn performance. He did. He devastated them. Miss Ruth wept for days. Ted was in a rage. Hadn't they, through their own prestige, their personal power, their potential advertising value to the press, their insistence, made possible Martin's job? They felt so. They saw him biting the hand that had fed him.

The final Denishawn triumph was the Carnegie Hall gala in April.

In early September Ruth St. Denis and Ted Shawn with nine Deni-shawn Dancers set out on an exhausting tour as stars of the *Ziegfeld Follies*, and they did not return to New York until the end of May 1928. What with frequent two-a-day shows and very often nine per-formances a week, they racked up more than three hundred perfor-mances on this tour! While they were gone, they left the Denishawn School in New York in the care of Humphrey and Weidman and an assisting faculty. Humphrey, ever loyal to Miss Ruth, was nonethe-less restless and she got Charles restless too. They had been infected by Martha's experiments, and although they were long-time col-leagues rather than continuously close friends of Graham's, they were excited by her rebellion. Years later Doris told me, "I just got tired of being Siamese, Burmese, Japanese and all the other 'eses.' I came from Oak Park, Illinois, and I wanted to find out as a dancer who I was, what Oak Park and I had to say in dance."

So Doris and Charles began experimenting at Denishawn. The bosses were away and they were in charge. Anyway, outside the standard curriculum, they were free to experiment. It never occurred to them at the time that they would follow Martha and leave Deni-shawn. Naïvely, perhaps, they assumed that they could work within Denishawn, that St. Denis and Shawn would incorporate their slowly evolving techniques within the Denishawn format, and that they would be encouraged to go ahead, to choreograph to bring something new to Denishawn. They did not take into account Shawn's Prussian attitude of command or his ego. St. Denis might not have been interested and quite probably would have actively disliked the young moderns' starkness of movement, their unadorned motions and emotions, but she probably would have said, "Oh, let them try out what they want to do." Shawn, however, was furious when he returned to Denishawn. They had been "vipers" in the breast of Denishawn, they had undermined him with the pupils and the nontouring Denishawners while he was away. Denishawn, under him, was perfect and, under him, would become more perfect in the future. There were meetings, stormy sessions, recriminations, and Doris, against her will, had to leave, taking Charles with her. There was no other course.

But it was while Doris and Charles were running the Denishawn School that John Martin seriously began to study contemporary dance. He listened to them, saw what they were doing, and he believed in them. He believed in Martha too, as well as the lesser ones just starting out in this new form. He espoused their cause. He thought it time to lay Denishawn to rest. Ten years later Miss Ruth forgave him and all the moderns, although she never liked modern dance as such, and the moderns came to look upon her as a rather glamorous, flighty, but charming ancestress. Ted bore the grudge against Martin all his life. It was at best an armed truce between them.

But that closing night at Carnegie was without a hint of decline. Indeed, expansion of Denishawn was very much in evidence—Ruth announced it in a curtain speech, while at the very same time destroying whatever was left of Ted's patience and willingness to put up with her by the arrogance of that speech. Earlier, when the Judson tour was in progress, she had announced it would be her last for a long time. She was not a robot. She needed rest. She needed peace. She needed love. She needed understanding. She needed to find her soul. But as the curtain closed on an ovation at Carnegie, Ruth St. Denis took a solo curtain call. She held up her hand. The audience quieted. She spoke her gratitude and went on to say that the audiences' years of faith in her would now enable her to fulfill *her* dream of a Greater Denishawn. With their faith *she* would see to the building of a great Denishawn House, America's first, specially designed home for dance in New York. She asked for support for *her* dream. She never mentioned Ted Shawn.

When the applause subsided, she returned to the wings. Her husband, who had dreamed of this Denishawn, was standing there. He was hurt and he was furious. She wrote, "In looking back on that night, I realize that I did an unforgivable thing, but my innocence was quite genuine at the time. . . . I apparently gave the impression that I had borne and sustained the whole Denishawn School unaided. . . . I had presented myself in the guise of the solitary head of this whole organization . . . the damage done became irreparable. I do not mean to imply that Ted was so unreasonable that this breach could not have been healed; but this situation was a symbol of what in retrospect appears as a necessary stage in the fully rounded development of us both . . . but the reverberations of that speech echoed in our lives until the end of Denishawn."

But Denishawn House, nevertheless, was begun. Brother St. Denis, many years before, had purchased some property for his sister in Van Cortlandt Park. When the idea for Denishawn House in New York City became firmly agreed upon, by Shawn at least, on the Judson tour, he had purchased some adjoining lots and the site was settled. Every cent they had earned and were earning was poured, along with the concrete, into the building.

The ground level was so designed that trucks could drive into it and deposit scenery and costumes for storage on that floor. It also had space for costume workshops, laundry and dyeing vats. Adjacent was a vault, which was planned for housing the vast accumulation of Denishawn records. The next floor had a studio two stories high, offices, reception room, and dining room. Over the nonstudio section were two bedrooms and two baths for St. Denis and Shawn, for this was to be their home. A stairway led to a tower, the library, and to the roof with its view of the park and what was left of the old Van Cortlandt estate. There were also further dreams—of a building with a dance theater and multiple studios for the school, but although St. Denis, after the separation, tried to raise funds for it, it remained a dream.

The *Follies* tour, which paid them $3,500 a week for nine months, was essential if Denishawn House was to be realized. Indeed, when it was built and the press assembled, St. Denis was asked to make a statement. Everyone expected a poetic, perhaps metaphysical, comment. The great lady placed her hand against the building and said, "Every brick a one-night stand."

It was on the *Follies* tour that they met and both came to enjoy an attractive young man. The three-way friendship grew and changed. Both St. Denis and Shawn found strong sexual attraction to him. This was not a new experience for St. Denis, but for Shawn, if his words to me and to others are to be believed, it was the first time he had established a more than casual physical relationship with another man. The rivalry became intense, for the young man had become a part of the Denishawn enterprise. Ruth knew what was happening. Ted found a letter in her handwriting addressed to his new love. He opened it. He tried to excuse his act later, but the truth was that he had to know. There was a terrible confrontation. St. Denis wrote:

"Our final dénouement came on one awful night in Denishawn House . . . the three years which followed were a period of blackness. . . . I stood in the ruins of my world. . . ."

Ted said, "I am frank and honest. I became absolutely infatuated with him, and by this I mean it was a strong overwhelming sexual attraction. . . . I realized that [he] was not going to be faithful to anyone. His friends, and by friends I mean the people he slept with, ranged from famous Broadway producers and their wives, sleeping with both of them . . . and sometimes these things hurt. . . ." But when it came to the lad and Ruth, it was too much.

Shawn told me that it was then St. Denis threatened to divorce him, naming the mutual lover as corespondent. If she had, his career, in that era, would have been destroyed. But she was prevailed upon to let her threat go unacted. She rushed off to California and left Denishawn to her husband, whom she never did divorce.

A happier, more helpful, and longer-lasting friendship was contracted on the *Follies* tour at almost the same moment. On the beach in Corpus Christi, Texas, where the Denishawners were sunning themselves briefly between performances, a lively young lady came up, stood on her head, and asked, "Can you do this?" It was a newspaper woman named Fern Helscher who became, a few years later, the devoted ally of Ted Shawn in his history-making era with the Men Dancers. She was instrumental in making that whole venture not only a national but an international success, and she did it out of love and enthusiasm and faith, for at first there was no pay and little food. But Fern, who stood on her head for Shawn, stood by him for years until she was no longer useful to him and she could be in his often-used word "released."

After the *Follies* tour the principals understandably began to go their separate ways. There were some final commitments. They gave their second Lewisohn Stadium performance in the summer of 1928 and took to the road for a handful of performances that fall. Another handful had been booked for the spring of 1929, but for the rest, Ted performed with the Denishawn Dancers in eight performances on the East Coast and with two musicians (the Khariton Duo) in a single performance at Carnegie, and St. Denis, sharing a program with the musical Concert Trio, gave a single in Los Angeles.

The third Lewisohn engagement came in the summer of 1929, and from October through January of 1930, there was a duet tour for St. Denis and Shawn. They lived separately but danced together, both realizing that it was all over but the echoes. The stock market crashed during the tour and with it, the gate receipts fell off sharply. The two had no desire to continue together for any longer than their contracts specified, yet separately, managers could not hope to book them, especially in depression times, as successfully as they had in the past when they were joint stars of a great company. There was a Lewisohn in the summer of 1931 and a fifth and final appearance of Ruth St. Denis, Ted Shawn, and their Denishawn Dancers in three performances at the Stadium August 24, 26, and 28, 1931. The last look that the thousands jamming the Stadium had of the two together—and they had danced together steadily since 1922 and originally since 1914—was in a romantic duet. It was called *Idyll*.

The idyll was on the program only. The final break in the marriage had come earlier, and Shawn had begun a new life pattern with the male lover. Was this sudden? If Shawn's homosexuality was latent, why had it been suppressed for so long? What was he looking for in a woman that he never found? Shawn himself had told me that he "guessed" homosexuality was always there "deep down." But he was concerned only with the "rightness" of homosexuality for those who wished that life style and were concerned with the homosexual's rights in society. And as I've said, he always put the "blame" for his switch on Ruth St. Denis, for he believed or wished to believe that if she had been a good wife, he would never have turned to another male for sexual fulfillment.

An opinion on his placement of blame for the failure of his marriage seemed to me to be worth seeking from a competent authority. I turned, as I have mentioned, to Dr. Girard Franklin, a psychologist and psychoanalyst who had actually been a dance student of Ted Shawn's for a summer at Shawn's Jacob's Pillow Dance Festival and School. Dr. Franklin, of course, does not believe in long-distance analysis, but he was willing to speculate. As a youth right out of military service (where he had served in the medical corps), Franklin had come to Jacob's Pillow to study dancing not as a vocation but as an avocation. He did not come to know Shawn well on a personal basis, but he knew him as a teacher, as a director, as a performer, and as the charismatic host at the Pillow.

Dr. Franklin also spent many hours reading my voluminous notes and discussing with me in detail the story of Ted Shawn. He remembered that Shawn had been fascinated when he read Franklin's student application for attendance at Jacob's Pillow because it had stated that the young man was studying psychology at college. With hours of coresearch and discussion with me on the Shawn family background, Dr. Franklin noted: "The connection between the relationship which Ted Shawn had with his mother and the relationship he had with Miss Ruth deserves consideration. Obviously his mother's death came at a very crucial time in his life. And living under the shadow of his superior, athletically superior, brother was also an element. But his mother's death must have been a profound loss, for she seemed to understand and encourage Ted's theatrical leanings. It is hard for us to know what his mother was like and what he had to do to please her, to woo her, as it were. Reading your notes, I see that he must have been deeply attached to her and that after her death he went into a deep period of depression. And I would think it played a very important part in his relationship to Miss Ruth.

"He related to Miss Ruth as to the older woman, for in many ways she seems to have been a replacement for his mother. Reading about Shawn and St. Denis you see time and time again that he needed her approval, just like any boy with his mother. He even sat at her feet like a child. I think one of the many stresses in their relationship was that he was seeking a maternal figure and, God! she was anything *but* a maternal figure. She didn't even want children of her own.

"This certainly played a part in the unhappiness he experienced in their relationship, and I think it does account for why he would, after that experience, give up on trying to form another relationship with a woman." Dr. Franklin goes on to postulate that perhaps young Ted's mother was not a doting mother, that she possibly had other interests or was not by nature a motherly mother, a good mother but not an exceptionally loving one. Therefore when Ted could not, he felt, please her or later his substitute mother, St.

Denis, he turned to young men to give them that love that he felt had been denied him.

Dr. Franklin told me how clearly he remembered his first reactions to Ted Shawn at Jacob's Pillow: "I was just a kid then, but I was most aware of his vulnerability. I think I knew then that his attitude of dominance was protective. I don't think I was much more than nineteen, perhaps twenty, but I felt instinctively that I should protect him. He was remote, aloof, and I think it was because he was insecure. I'm quite sure that he could have made a career without Miss Ruth—he was adventurous, successful—but neurotically he needed her. He was hooked. He adored her like a child adores his beautiful mother. Her approval was the key to his own confidence in himself. He didn't get it from her. I would guess he didn't get it from his mother. Where could he turn next?"

He hungered for approval from women, Dr. Franklin felt, while at the same time protecting himself from them.

Some weeks after my talk with Dr. Franklin, I came upon a folder of typed material that Shawn had given me for eventual use in my biography of him. I was stunned to come across something I had previously overlooked. Ted Shawn had written: "The death of [brother] Arnold and what followed profoundly influenced my life. Because not only was he my idol and my god, so loving, so kind, so beautiful in character, so beautiful in body, but he was the first-born. After he died, it was as if someone had laid an axe to my mother's taproot. You could see the top withering. She lived only eight months.

"I want to go on with the effect on me. It wasn't for some time that I realized the power of the first-born, especially if it's a son, over the mother. At first I was numb with grief. I had two deaths so close to me in my own family, and the drownings of three cousins and not too long after that my father's remarriage. And then I was living alone. Gradually, the reaction came. It was based on the sense of comparison. My mother didn't love me as much as she loved my brother. This was quite true. It wasn't that she didn't love me but I kept feeling 'Well, but Mama, you have *me*, you still have *me*.' But it didn't mean anything that she had a husband and a home and another son. She went out in only eight months.

"This I think has been a trauma long buried that may have had some bearing on some of my overt misbehavior in my life. I don't know . . . that feeling of not actually being rejected but not being worth living for. . . ."

Through the years this haunted and disturbed Ted Shawn. The St. Denis substitute failed. The female had failed. The false idyll was over.

In 1928, Ted had opened a studio of his own, the Japanese Studio in Westport, Connecticut. It was Japanese in design and St. Denis helped him dedicate it 'with pertinent Japanese ceremonies. But it was his. Also his were two solo tours of Europe in 1930 and 1931. He was soloist at the Third German Dance Congress in Munich in *Orpheus Dionysos*, choreographed by the great Mary Wigman's close associate Margrethe Wallman. In his own recitals he was enormously successful. At the close of his dance *Frohsinn*, he received forty-seven curtain calls in Munich. In telling of his triumph there he would always add, "I didn't go over as well in Cologne. Only twenty-seven calls!" *Frohsinn*, a ballet-rooted but barefooted warm-up exercise, got into the repertory by chance. It was 1931 and in Germany. Katherine Dreier, an abstract painter (she did an "abstract psychological portrait" of Shawn which was reproduced in her book *Shawn the Dancer*) and an ardent admirer, told him that his last number before intermission should be light and happy. She explained that Germans wanted it that way so that they would be in a carefree frame of mind for their coffee and pastries at the interval. Shawn had only his *Flamenco Dances* to fill that need, and he wanted them for his finale. Miss Dreier suggested the dance she saw him do in rehearsal. He explained that it was not a dance but an exercise, a bunch of steps he had strung together to prepare for a performance. Besides, he had no costume. Miss Dreier insisted. "It's joyous. Call it *Frohsinn* after the Lincke music. Wear your warm-up dress." He did as he was told. The result was a smashing success not only in Germany but back in America for a few seasons until he was no longer agile enough to do it with the easy joy that Dreier had savored. At its première, he was already forty years old.

On his return a winter (1931–1932) tour had been booked for Ted Shawn and His Dancers. It opened December 4 in Williamstown, not far from his newly acquired farm, Jacob's Pillow, nine miles east of Lee, Massachusetts, and it closed on March 1 in Eustis, Florida, where he would have his winter home and where he would die nearly forty years later. On January 7, 1932, in Chapel Hill, North Carolina, when I saw him dance for the first time, all I remember from the program was *Frohsinn*, four boys doing an Indian dance (*Osage-Pawnee Dance of Greeting*) and the boys and girls in *Boston Fancy—1854*. To me, at the time, it was just another event on the university's student entertainment series—I was much more excited about Amelita Galli-Curci's concert—but I enjoyed it and dutifully went backstage, as we did for all such events, and collected autographs. The most important one was not Shawn's. It was Phoebe Baughan. A year later she would be living in Chapel Hill, introducing me to dance and, with that introduction, leading me into a way of life and a career I had never anticipated, and . . . introducing me to the first star I had ever met, Ted Shawn.

11

Phoebe began it all for me. Looking back I'm faced with a series of fascinating "ifs." If one of those "ifs" had failed, I'm not at all certain that I would have ever come to know Ted Shawn or, indeed, have become a dance critic. If Phoebe Baughan had not married E. Scott Barr; if Scott had not insisted that she quit touring and be with him; if he had not been a physicist; if he had not received an appointment at the University of North Carolina; if I had not been a student at UNC; if Phoebe hadn't gotten restive there and decided to teach some dance at Chapel Hill; if my roommate had not said to me, "There's a faculty wife teaching dancing to girls; shall we go and see what it's all about?" would I have ever found dance? I like to think I would have come to it some other way. But the fact is that Foster Fitz-Simons and I said, "Let's try it."

I remember our first class. It was on the second floor of the Student Union building on campus. Phoebe made us stretch, twist, flex, reach, jump, and what not. After class was over Foster and I started downstairs. My legs gave out and I slid into a heap at the bottom. I looked up at Foster and said, "This is it." I never changed my mind. Dance was it for me. It became so for Foster. It also grabbed some other boys on campus in a day when dancing for men was what was called "anathema."

Neither Foster nor I were weaklings. I didn't collapse at the knees because I had never exercised. Indeed, as I already mentioned, I not only took gym classes to which I was assigned, I took classes for other boys who hated gymnasium. I usually took two gym classes a day. I almost always saw Foster on the indoor track above while we were on the ground level doing side-straddle-hops, lifting dumbbells, touching toes, running in place, grunting over pushups and situps, and sometimes ending with wrestling. Foster was a runner. Later, after we had started working with Phoebe, Foster and I, after four hours of class and rehearsals with our growing group of boys and girls, would run the mile outdoors in the stadium. So I think my falling downstairs in spite of my good athletic conditioning made me respect dance, physically.

Phoebe was a product of Ted Shawn rather than of Ruth St. Denis. She had had lessons, of course, from Miss Ruth at Denishawn, but she was mainly Shawn-taught, and because she had performed with his non-Denishawn group, she was closer to him personally. She adored him and she instilled that adoration into us. She was tiny and very southern, but she was both strong of character and strong in movement. She was therefore very good for boys who were beginning to dance at a time when the word for men who danced was simply "sissy." If she had been a willowy St. Denis type, she would have been bad for us. Indeed, male dance instructors are much better than female ones for boys who are starting to dance because as one is learning one mimics. But Phoebe herself was best at dances that were characterized by strong movement attack, sustained intensities. She was utterly feminine but not interested in classical ballet. She gave us primitive rhythms which she had learned in class from Shawn, she taught us movements which Shawn either used in his dances or in preparation for his dances. She had also found rapport with the modern dance technique of Germany's major modern dance pioneer, Mary Wigman. This had come to her by way of Margrethe Wallman, Wigman's assistant, the choreographer of the *Orpheus* production in which Ted had danced and the last major teaching import at Denishawn. The Wigman technique, rooted in the principle of tension relaxation and the gradations between the two extremes—muscle inertness to muscle explosion—was not only a good base for her own dramatic dances but also virile material for us.

We started making programs right away. Phoebe did a lot of the choreography, but she let us have a hand too. Foster was instantly the most prolific here, showing a choreographic bent that would lead him, along with his partner-to-be, Miriam Winslow, to considerable fame. Naturally we did a music visualization. But we also danced Negro spirituals, very dear to Phoebe's heart—she sang them well and danced them beautifully—and we did little numbers to songs like "At the Bend of the River" and "Shortnin' Bread." Foster did a really beautiful dance—he composed the score also—based on the ancient Easter Trope, the seed of English drama in the Middle Ages, in which the three Marys, acted by three monks, come to the tomb of Christ and are met by the Angel, also a monk. The four leading boys of the group—Foster, Harry Coble, Fred Howard, and I—danced it. Of the four I always did and still do place myself last, but Phoebe in an interview a few years ago with a university student who had selected me as the subject of her dissertation for her doctorate, placed me number two. The other three, however, ultimately appeared with Ted Shawn and his Men Dancers. I never did. I was invited to join, as I've said, but I was determined then as always to be a writer. But it was nice to be asked, although I was reasonably certain then (and now) that Shawn made the invitation mainly because Foster and I were close friends in college, and he thought we were so deeply involved in dance that we'd like to go on with it together.

Shawn understood my decision to stay at school instead. It was made on a purely practical basis. This was the Great Depression, jobs were hard to come by, Foster and I got through on scholarships and not very much to eat, and in those days a college degree could almost always assure you of a teaching job or, in business, a better position. Today, outside the field of education, I don't think degrees matter much. I was never asked if I had a diploma, although I had it at the ready when applying for newspaper positions.

Shawn, however, encouraged me continuously in my ambition to be a dance critic. I remember one Thanksgiving in Chapel Hill. Shawn and his boys had played Memorial Hall on campus. Phoebe and Scott had a party. I hardly remember who was there in the little house. But it was a great moment for me. Ted Shawn was sitting in the most comfortable chair in the room as befitted the guest of honor. Somewhere along the line I wound up sitting at his feet—not out of adulation, although I would have been happy to adulate, if there is such a word, but because Phoebe had run out of chairs—and I told him about my writing interests.

He knew from Phoebe that I was a reporter and an occasional interviewer (I remember I interviewed the Belgian ambassador) and critic (I reviewed some events in our college entertainment series) for the university newspaper, the *Daily Tar Heel.* Foster and I also wrote for the very literary *Carolina Magazine;* he with some very beautiful poems and I with a pretty carefully researched article designed to strip the mantle of righteousness from an almost sacred gentleman in the university's history, together with a series of three-line Japanese poems called Hokkus (spelled "haiku" nowadays).

I think I told him that I came from a family with lots of writers—a grandfather who was an editor on the *New York World* and the *Brooklyn Eagle,* and who did publicity for both Buffalo Bill and Rudyard Kipling; an uncle who wrote some of the "Boy Scouts in . . ." whatever location he could dream up; and a great aunt who, under the name of Sophie May, had written an endless array of "Little Prudy" and "Dottie Dimple" books (for children, you'll be happy to know).

From that day in 1933 until his death just a fraction under forty years later I don't believe he missed reading a word—millions of them—I wrote. Although he was a very accomplished writer himself, he was of no influence whatsoever on me in terms of the craft of writing. But at the beginning and for several years to come he exerted a strong influence on my dance tastes and esthetics. It had to be that way because I didn't know anything at all about dance other than what he told me or what Phoebe taught me, and she, of course, was governed largely by his tastes, although she was quietly much more involved with modern dance than she ever seemed to let on to him.

But we were all, at first, pretty much antiballet. We didn't know any better. Our instructors were echoing the battle against the old-time ("moribund" was Miss Ruth's word) ballet that Isadora, Miss Ruth, and later Ted had met and countered with the "new" dance. A new ballet age, in 1933, had just begun, but Ted was not about to admit it. He was still espousing his theory that "Russian" ballet could never truly reflect America. Martha and Doris and Charles and, indeed, all the rebellious young moderns who were spurning Denishawn were also spurning ballet. Martha, at a lecture, had already exchanged condemnations with Michel Fokine.

Fokine, choreographer of *Petrouchka, Scheherezade, Prince Igor* and other major ballets, had himself been a rebel within the field of ballet. He had been inspired by Isadora Duncan at the turn of the century, and since he was not permitted to jolt the staid Russian Imperial Ballet, he had found creative outlet with Serge Diaghilev's Ballets Russes, which had burst like rockets over Paris and, indeed the Western world, from 1909 to 1929 when the great impresario, Diaghilev, died. Martha knew of Fokine's reputation, but she had not recognized him when, at her lecture, he rose from the audience to defend ballet against her diatribe.

Ted and Miss Ruth, Martha and all the other moderns were certainly more respectful of Fokine than of old Marius Petipa (creator of *The Sleeping Beauty* and other Russian ballet classics) and his imitators. But even if they saw Fokine as an innovator, they were convinced that ballet was foreign and always would be. Even John Martin agreed. He could not accept at first—he changed his mind drastically in later years—the concept of an American ballet. The fact that Denishawn danced exotica from the Orient was explained by saying that if you were an American dancer what you danced was American and that the Denishawners used their own techniques in adapting foreign themes to the American theater. Ballet in the minds of American dancers—and the American public too—in the 1920s was a Russian affair.

Shawn took great delight in telling us that when he started out as a professional dancer, some rich ladies (he always attracted ladies, rich or poor) wanted to pay his way to Russia to study ballet because they said he would never be a success if he were not a Russian-trained ballet dancer. He declined, vowed he'd become world famous as a dancer in his own dance way, and reported that it was not long before he could say he was far more famous in America than any other male dancer.

Ted, when he began with the men's group, was supermasculine. There was no ballet *port-de-bras* with lyrical arms and elegant hands. Quite a number of the Shawn dances, in fact, used fists. I hasten to say that although there were many American Communists during the depression era, the Shawn fist was not of the "Workers party" variety; to the contrary, he once said to me, half in jest and half seriously, that he was probably the only living American who thought Herbert Hoover was our greatest president. The fists, the bulging biceps, the concentration on muscular themes—war dances, labor dances, sports dances—were very necessary when I first began to dance. Classical ballet, even to those of us who had become students of dance, did seem effeminate. I was even smart aleck enough to write a satire on the newly arrived Ballet Russe de Monte Carlo and call it the Charlotte Russe, a dessert concocted almost entirely with whipped cream.

It wasn't until later that I realized that the elegance of ballet was not sissified, that ballet had been created by and for courtiers, and that men with lace at their wrists in attendance to their king might well go forth the next morning, sword in hand, to do battle for their king and country. The etiquette of the court had simply become the convention, the style of ballet. Americans, in 1776, had disposed of a royal court and courtiers, so it was natural that a rough and rude people, for generations to come, would look with suspicion on anything which harked of palaces. American men would not enjoy the respect and honor they have earned today as dancers in ballet if their battles had not been fought decades before by Ted Shawn and succeeding moderns who accented, even overaccented, virile movements, a dance style evolved from natural body movements and not from gestures and steps which had been born on gleaming ballroom floors.

We should have recognized all this then but we did not, and Shawn was of no help in trying to strike down prejudices against men in ballet. For the times Shawn was right. He was also the ideal type of male to proclaim the masculinity of male dance. His homosexual side was latent during all but the last days of Denishawn, and his acceptance of his homosexuality was known only to a few and, perhaps, to theater people—but not to the public. He was big and husky and in no way slight and lithe as are most male ballet dancers. In fact his body was far from the ideal dancer's body. He was never very limber, and what virtuosity he achieved—and he was far more virtuosic than his wife—was based on strength and force rather than on finesse.

Offstage he was charming. Not only did women adore him, but ordinary men liked him instantly, for although he was an artist, he was a shrewd businessman, he could talk male talk, he was interested in politics, world affairs, science, if not sports. Yes, he was right for his day, and what he did, although it might seem to us superbutch for our day, was absolutely essential. If he couldn't get dance into a college, he damn well got rhythmic gymnastics into the curriculum, even though the teaching was exactly the same—he knew how to play the semantic game.

Phoebe did give us a little of what was called free-style ballet, the kind I have described in Shawn's *Frohsinn*. It was done barefoot. We were always barefoot in Shawn-style dance or in modern. Still, we did turns and *glissades* and picked up splinters and split our feet and got so that our calluses were thick enough to put out cigarettes with our bare feet.

I once stepped on a piece of broken glass from a spotlight just before I went on stage in some primitive dance, and with a glass shard in my heel I did a toe-heel-stomp in exquisite agony: I loved the show-must-go-on chance it gave me! Later, when Foster was on tour, he split open the sole of his foot and it became infected. This was before penicillin and antibiotics. He soaked it after every performance and somehow managed to avoid blood poisoning, but the thing healed with a big cleft in the sole of his foot. Sometime later Harry Coble nearly lost a leg from blood poisoning. Still and all we practiced *fouettés* (continuous turns on one foot) on awful floors, barefoot. Marion Tatum, who later became Mrs. Fitz-Simons, was one of our top dancers, and she used to tear her flesh on that Memorial stage where we'd hold our four-hour classes. About twenty years later, when I was visiting Chapel Hill, I went to Marion's spot—we all had places where we practiced turns and the like, and the blood stain was still there. We were proud of it.

To appreciate Ted Shawn's incalculable contribution not only to male dance in America but to American dance itself it is essential to look at it in the light of its times. I can do that because I was there. Today Nureyev, Baryshnikov, and many others in ballet and in modern dance are superstars—it is almost a male-star age in dance— but what male dance star did we have in the first three decades of this century? No one but Ted Shawn in that field we call the art dance (it was "interpretive" way back then). Ah, yes, in show biz, there were the great hoofers, the tap dancers, the black dancers, the eccentric dancers. But that was it. Shawn stood alone and won acceptance. But his second job was to win acceptance for other males. With his Men Dancers that's what he set out to do. He succeeded.

We can find lots that is obvious, corny, even of questionable esthetic value today. But back then . . . I remember in January of 1935 I hitchhiked from Chapel Hill to Greensboro (where the women's branch of the university was located) to see Foster dance with the men's group. Before the performance I saw him. He was excited about my seeing him for the first time with the Shawn troupe, but he was scared to death because his father would be in the audience. Foster's brother had been a star football player and was now in the respectable insurance business. The other son had become a dancer! No wonder he was worried. But after the performance Mr. Fitz-Simons went backstage to see his boy. He said with approval, "Well, son, you worked hard." Sweat streaming from his body Foster grinned, looked at me quickly, and we both knew that he hadn't been expelled from a fine Atlanta family.

Not long after I came to know Shawn, he began to send me clippings of reviews or, in his letters, quotes from the press. A writer, assigned to cover a performance on the first tour, said in advance, "Must be a bunch of pansies." But after an interview and a look at the performance he wrote, "No pansies they—these men, their work being of a most difficult type . . . demands the respect of even the most accomplished athlete. . . . I left that night wholly in sympathy with the movement to advance the Manly Art of Dancing." And another: "Last evening was a triumph indeed for Ted Shawn and his ideal of an all-male dance program."

Those who approved used words like "he-man," "rugged," "hair-on-the-chest" dancing; even John Martin admitted that it was "highly important that capable male dancers be developed." Martin had strong reservations about the dances themselves and especially about the scantiness of the costumes. The minimal costume—the briefest of trunks and sometimes not much more than a posing strap—bothered others also. A few, while agreeing that the boys were muscular and virile, clear-eyed and apparently straight, couldn't understand why they wanted to switch their athleticism for dancing, since dancing, to them, was a matter of swans and nymphs. And there were those who felt that although Ted Shawn himself was an exception to the rule that dance was for the ladies, he was misguided in his belief that his "personal genius" could be transferred to others.

But in the main the American press, even in rural and conservative areas, gave the project support. And this support came not only from ordinary reporters but also from thoughtful, knowledgeable critics and essayists. Lucien Price of the *Boston Globe* was a philosopher and a scholar. As Shawn was starting out on the male venture, he related Shawn to Emerson's *Shakespeare, The Poet* in quoting, "He is isolated among his contemporaries, by truth and by his art, but with this consolation in his pursuits, that they will draw all men sooner or later."

Price was present at the first all-male Shawn concert, March 21, 1933, at the Repertory Theater in Boston. This was one of three programs which Shawn and his dancers—a mixed company of men and women—were giving in Boston. The all-men program was the experiment. Price was so impressed that, although he had never met Ted Shawn, he wrote him a long letter a week after attending the event. He commented on the dances, the philosophies behind some of the choreography, the technique, the purpose, the importance of the venture and even suggested music that Shawn might use for future numbers.

Price wrote: "The dancing of the young men was boldly original, even in the pieces when they danced with women, for their masculinity was much more sharply differentiated than is usual. I do not recall that even the Russians ever brought it off quite like this. Perhaps the flavor of something exotic and oriental in the Russian dancing puts us off; but in your company, for the first time, as it seemed to me, I saw young Americans dancing *as* Americans and dancing in an art-form."

Price went on to speak of his research into ancient Greek dances for men, dance led by the handsome, teen-age Sophocles, dances for nude athlete-warriors. He discussed the esthetic and emotional values, as well as the physical virtues, of dance for men: "We Americans, and especially our young men, need emotional and mental release through an art-form. The trouble has been that our race is predominent in men of action. The fellow who wields brush, pen, piano or fiddlebow is, among us, a white blackbird. But the dance is an art-form for men of action. In fact it always has been since the dawn of time."

The two soon met and established a friendship that lasted for the rest of their lives, and it found its particular flowering in an exchange of letters that encompassed the seven-year duration of the men's group. The letters continued beyond that, of course, for both were prolific writers and ardent corresponders, but the bond was men in the arts and especially in dance.

For this first program Shawn was able to augment the male nucleus in the mixed group with some of his students from Springfield College in nearby Springfield, Massachusetts, not far from his farm, Jacob's Pillow. He had been engaged by the college, a YMCA school, to teach dancing for men beginning in January of that year. Barton Mumaw had been with his troupe; now from Springfield came Wilbur McCormack and Frank Overlees to participate in the historic première—and to remain with the company throughout its life-span. Other young athletes joined in the years that followed, for it was part of Shawn's shrewd plan to publicize the fact that his boys were mainly university lettermen excelling in such masculine sports as boxing, wrestling, swimming, decathlon. Dennis Landers, a member of the first men's group (following the Boston preview), actually had a pole-vault record which remained unbroken for several years. Mary Campbell, piano accompanist for Shawn on his solo tours abroad, at home, and for the Boston season, left when the permanent male troupe was established. She helped Shawn to find a male successor in the person of Jess Meeker, who became not only the accompanist but also the composer for the company.

The first performances were held in the summer of 1933 at Jacob's Pillow. With his new company Shawn began rehearsing his program. F. Cowles Strickland, director of the nearby Berkshire Playhouse in Stockbridge, suggested that some of the rehearsals be opened to the public for a small admission charge. Shawn didn't think anyone would come, but he tried it and about fifty people showed up at seventy-five cents apiece. He talked about dance and his goals, the boys served tea and danced, the audience sat on the floor at one end of the barn converted into studio. For some of the heftier Berkshire dowagers who adored Shawn, loved Barton, and appreciated the nearly nude boys, camp chairs were provided. These were the modest antecedents of what was to become the most famous dance festival in the world, the Jacob's Pillow Dance Festival.

It was not called a festival in 1933. They were simply "the teas."

The summer of 1940, when the men's group was disbanded, Mary Washington Ball, a dance educator and physical education director at the New York State Normal School in Cortland, New York, leased the Pillow and established the Jacob's Pillow School of Dance and Festival. (Ted was engaged simply to teach some classes.) It was she who coined the name. In 1941 the great ballet stars Alicia Markova and Anton Dolin leased the place and, with members of The Ballet Theatre (now the American Ballet Theatre), opened an International Dance Festival and School. Again, Shawn was an employee, a guest artist. And in the fall of 1941 Shawn sold Jacob's Pillow to a group who formed a corporation as the Jacob's Pillow Dance Festival, Inc., and, in turn, engaged Shawn to direct it, run it, manage it, and, after some maneuverings in matters of board membership, to boss the enterprise and do exactly as he pleased.

For a while he gave credit to Miss Ball for founding the festival, but in due course, her contribution was forgotten, and on letterheads and all publicity Ted Shawn was listed not simply as director but as "founder-director." This wasn't an isolated instance of taking full credit for something that required shared credit. A book of Denishawn-Shawn anecdotes, published by Doubleday under the title *1001 Night Stands*, was written with Mrs. Gray Poole, who had taken Shawn's 600,000-word autobiography in manuscript, extracted the anecdotes, and rewritten much of it. The book proper and the jacket made it clear that Mrs. Poole, a professional writer and publicist long associated with dance through her husband, Lynn Poole, himself a onetime Denishawn dancer, a Johns Hopkins staff member, a brilliantly pioneering television producer, was the coauthor. This was a book I was supposed to have done in collaboration with Shawn but never did—and more of that anon. But soon after publication, with Gray being praised for her brilliant editing, Ted began to skip over her name and before long it was his book exclusively.

I hope it is clear that Shawn's assumption of accomplishments not totally his own was not the result of plotting. By saying often enough what he wished had happened, he came to believe that it was true. He could have taken a lie-detector test about the festival and the book, stated that he was wholly responsible for both and come through with flying colors. He believed what he wanted to believe. When he got rid of someone, it didn't take him long to truly believe he had released the person to do what he wanted to do unhampered in any way by him. He was, in his own mind, totally unselfish.

He did in truth put Jacob's Pillow on the map, and his modest lecture-demonstrations did eventually lead to the Jacob's Pillow Dance Festival. After all, his courage and his vision were of phenomenal caliber, equal to his very robust ego.

He had done his 1933 repertory week in Boston not only during the Depression but during the Bank Holiday (when no one could take money out) declared by President Roosevelt to save the nation from panic and bankruptcy. Yet his deficit was just a little more than twenty-five dollars. With America in desperate financial straits, he nonetheless planned his all-male troupe. It should be remembered that the public hadn't asked for any such thing. Only *he* wanted it and only *he* believed in it.

With some money earned by teaching and two solo appearances at a gala in Texas, he borrowed $1,500 and set out with his new company. It took courage, for the guarantees offered by local managers were very often minimal. I remember his telling me when I first met him in Chapel Hill that they had agreed to travel something like five hundred miles to a place that had guaranteed only a fifty dollar payment in the event that nobody bought any tickets. He gambled and the performance brought in several hundred at the box office, but there had been no assurance. The company traveled in one car and a truck. They set up a show with a ground cloth (this was long before the day of portable stage floors) where needed on splintery stages, with lights and what few props were required. They danced an entire program, packed the costumes, and moved on to the next booking. Often they drove all night. They played well over one hundred dates a tour.

Shawn did not drive. He said he didn't want to know how, and then he would always be driven. He sat in the front seat of the car next to the driver and discussed dance with the boys or read aloud. Dancers in his company were not permitted to be illiterate—no physically perfect but mentally limited creatures were tolerated.

In summers at the Pillow, at the lunch hour, the men of the company and male students sun-bathed nude outside the studio. Shawn read aloud. The reading materials were by no means trivia. During the Denishawn tours he and Miss Ruth would read not only from the mystic poets but also, say, Ouspensky's *Tertium Organum*. Essays on art and esthetics, physics and metaphysics, histories and biographies, all were food for student ears. Shawn, of course, would decide what was good for them and what was not. He would also state his opinions on subjects and his opinions were to be definitive. As I say, my friend Foster would rebel. I wasn't there on a day-to-day basis, but I'd get opinions through letters or during my summer visits to the Pillow. It was a kind of benevolent brainwashing.

By disparaging ballet he succeeded very well in convincing the boys that ballet was not for Americans, that it was European in origin and in continuing character. He was even more violent about the modern dancers, but there was, of course, personal animosity there for his disobedient Denishawn children. Still, the boys would sneak away to nearby Bennington College School of the Dance and the Bennington Dance Festival to have a forbidden peek at Martha, Doris, Charles, and Hanya Holm, who were the stars and apostles of modern dance there. The boys, quietly, found they liked a great deal that was going on at Bennington, but they were careful to keep quiet about it when in The Presence.

But Ted's aversion was by no means one-sided. The moderns were contemptuous of Ted Shawn. Martha, at an interview, had said that if one was speaking of artists the name of Ted Shawn would hardly come up. But the moderns at Bennington disliked each other too. That great dance educator and administrator Martha Hill, and her codirector at Bennington, Mary Josephine Shelley, staggered the opposing stars during the summer courses in order to keep them apart. Doris referred to Martha as a "snake," and Martha would cross the street rather than have to nod at Hanya. Each had a following which was as violently partisan as Shawn's own followers. Girls who studied at Bennington with Martha tried to look like her. Whether there was any physical resemblance or not did not matter. They would suck in their cheeks in an effort to get that primitive mask look, and their expressions were frozen into enigmatic mystery. I got on a bus once in North Adams and sat next to a girl with an inscrutable look. I said, "You must be a Graham student." She asked, "How did you know?" It was the same way, years before, when little girls came out of the local theater after seeing Gloria Swanson in a movie, they always seemed to have more teeth than when they went in.

The moderns not only disapproved of each other and of Shawn but, as I say, of ballet also. Graham students caught studying ballet were barred from Graham classes. Doris once said to me that Graham dancers could certainly not perform in Humphrey-Weidman technique and added, in an effort to be fair, that probably Humphrey-Weidman dancers would have difficulties with Graham technique. When I suggested that if such were the case, then her pupils' dance training must be very remiss because a mere ballet dancer could perform in Petipa and Fokine and Massine styles, each different from the other, do national dances, and in such avant-garde ballets as Massine's *Choreartium*, take off their shoes and move like modern dancers. Doris, always forthright and quick to agree if once convinced, said, "You're absolutely right. A dancer should be a dancer."

Today this attitude of narrowness seems hard to understand. Every dancer studies as many techniques as he can. He has got to be the kind of dancer I was suggesting to Doris—a total dancer. Graham and the other moderns even use ballet terms—a *plié* is much quicker to say and to comprehend than "kneebend"—interspersed with the anatomical or stylistic terminology of modern. A dancer, in today's ballet company repertory, must be able to do straight-out modern and jazz as well as classical ballet, and a dancer in show business for summer stock must be prepared to go from the classical ballet in *Song of Norway* to Oriental in *The King and I* or American Indian in *Annie Get Your Gun* to jazz in *West Side Story* or American folk in *Oklahoma!* In fact the American Ballet Theatre's Cynthia Gregory, before dancing *Swan Lake* or *Giselle*, warms up in the wings with a strictly classical ballet *barre*, but if she is to do Desdemona in José Limón's *The Moor's Pavane* (one of several modern dance works now in ballet repertory), she lies on the floor and warms up with modern dance stretches.

But in the 1930s it was pioneering time, and each pioneer was certain he had the right way. Besides, money was not to be had and jobs were scarce. When Weidman asked Harriette Ann Gray, a student at Bennington, if she would like to be in the Humphrey-

Weidman company, she was thrilled, but her practical parents had told her to always ask about salaries, so she said, "How much do you pay a performance?" "Ten dollars," said Charles. "And how often would I perform?" asked Harriette. "Maybe ten times a year," replied Charles. "How can I live on that?" asked Harriette. "Do you know how to run an elevator?" said Charles. "No," said Harriette. "Well, you'd better learn," suggested Charles. She did, and Harriette Ann Gray went on to become an important modern dancer and dance educator (the head of the prestigious dance department at Stephens College).

The moderns were jealous of each other and very envious of Shawn because their former boss, who should have been on the skids, was doing far better than they with one hundred and sometimes one hundred and fifty performances a year. Even John Martin, who was hardly a Shawn fan, duly reported the fact that no other dancer could boast a tour to match the Shawn seasons.

I don't believe Shawn himself ever visited Bennington. Miss Ruth did. Martha Hill made her a guest of honor, and when, at the corner coffee shop in North Bennington, Miss Ruth walked in the door with Martha Graham, all the Bennington students and faculty applauded. The rift, or half of it, was healed at that instant. Shawn was furious. To him it was dire plotting "in the enemy camp." Ruthie had been made a "tool." After all, he said, she was no rival to them any longer. She performed only sporadically and was concentrating in the 1930s on her Rhythmic Choir and her dance liturgies. By welcoming her he felt that the moderns were astutely admitting to their heritage but a heritage without him, one represented only by Miss Ruth. He was white with anger when he told me about it.

Miss Ruth, of course, was not fooled by it, for she had never forgotten what Martin had said about her and Denishawn, but the recognition made her the source of it all, it opened up possibilities of better coverage for her in the *New York Times* and, well, it couldn't hurt. Just a few years later I tried personally to extend the truce for Shawn's sake. I had just joined the staff of the *New York Herald Tribune*, and behind the scenes I arranged for a party at 110 East Fifty-ninth Street in the elaborate studio which had once belonged to Isadora Duncan, then to Miss Ruth, and was later to serve superbly for the School of Natya, headed by Miss Ruth and the great ethnic dance expert La Meri, and lastly as La Meri's own historic Ethnologic Dance Center. It was a nice party but tense. Miss Ruth floated about and was both suitably vague and utterly charming. Ted was on his best behavior. Martha and Doris and Charles came. It may well have been a sort of blackmail on my part, for I was the dance critic of a powerful newspaper, and I was an ardent supporter of modern dance and at the same time a believer in Ted Shawn's stature, in the Denishawn past, and in the importance of Men Dancers present.

We were all, along with other celebrated dancers, photographed for the *Times'* Sunday rotogravure section, which was *the* place to be in the Sunday *Times* for society, fashion, charity, and the arts. Yes, the roto was very big in those days. So we did indeed make news. I was then, and am now, amused by the fact that I was the only one in the picture (and I was centrally located) not identified in the caption. But then, the *Times* was careful to skirt the fact that the *Herald Tribune* had a dance critic.

The party went well, but it was no more than a surface truce. Behind the scenes vilification went on. Even when what seemed like a possible rapprochement was in the wind, Shawn would reject it. In 1939 he wrote to me that Doris, Charles, and Pauline turned up after a concert by the men's group at the Studebaker Theater in Chicago and "slobbered all over me."

The moderns were always "the enemy camp." Bennington closed down during World War II, but in 1948 it reopened, in a new place and in new guise but with the same adherence to modern dance principles, at the Connecticut College School of the Dance in New London. Ultimately Shawn was asked to lecture on his specialty, François Delsarte and the influence of Delsarte on dance. He was both excited and terrified, and although he'd given his Delsarte lecture untold times, he reworked it in detail. This time he planned to insert the facts: who had discovered Delsarte (he had), who was Delsarte's heir in adapting his principles to dance (he was), who had really founded American dance (he had).

I arrived at the Pillow to cover some performances and was summoned to the upstairs porch of the old farmhouse—the sanctum sanctorum—to hear a practice tape of what he was going to say. He would have a captive audience of modern dancers—his own rebellious children and their pupils and modern dance teachers from all over the United States—and he was going to let them know who he was and what he had accomplished and how he had never been given credit for what he had done, and he could prove it, so there! I listened to it and knew that he would crucify himself.

But how to tell him what to do? I thought quickly and grabbed at his cliché "the enemy camp." I said, "You know you're going into the enemy camp?" Yes he did. "Did it occur to you that this was to be a trap?" No, but it could be, it probably was, and did I have any suggestions? I did. I told him that listening to what he had prepared, I saw he had fallen right into the trap. They had invited him to come so that he would destroy himself because they hadn't been able to do the job themselves. So I urged him, "Don't dwell on yourself. Concentrate on dance. Say that you and Miss Ruth were pioneers and that what you had started in the wilderness, Martha and Doris and Charles extended beyond your and Miss Ruth's fondest hopes and wildest dreams." He looked at me. "Don't battle them. Disarm them," I said.

He listened to me. He trusted me. He knew that I had long supported his position in dance, without lauding every aspect of it and disapproving of much, and that I truly wanted the best for him. So he went to New London. I was in the audience. He charmed the pants off everyone there. He talked about Delsarte. He talked about Martha and Doris and Charles and how their accomplishments had left his far behind *but* that they too were being succeeded by still another generation who would surpass them. He was gently patriarchal, exuding affection and pride, naming Donald McKaye, a gifted black dancer, as one of his "talented grandchildren," comparing his rough pioneering efforts with the increasing masteries of those succeeding generations gathered there at all age levels in the college's Palmer Auditorium. He was a smashing success.

Doris, ever honest, came backstage, embraced him, and said, "Ted, I'm really ashamed. I had forgotten how much I had learned from you." More important was that all the students and the modern dance teachers from many colleges who had been hearing unflattering appraisals of Ted Shawn, funny but biting anecdotes and withering comments, succumbed to his charm and wondered what the hell all the venom had been about. They fell in love with him. They had long since accepted Miss Ruth; now they accepted him.

I raced back to the green room to congratulate him. He was white, shaking and perspiring. "I did what you said. I'll admit it worked. But it nearly killed me to say what I did about those bastards." It was, then, another great performance.

Life at the Pillow in the years of the men's group was rugged. The old colonial George Carter farm had been bought by Shawn as a sort of retreat. Because of a huge, sloping rock near the house, Shawn had named the place Jacob's Pillow. Nearby, the highest point in the Berkshires was called Jacob's Ladder, and there was also a Jacob's Well. The house had no heat, other than that provided by two big back-to-back fireplaces, one serving what was to be used as the parlor and the other, the company dining room. There was no running water either, but right outside the door was a well with sparkling water (used to this day). Shawn himself had an inside commode and a rigged-up shower that provided hot water. But the members of the company and the students had to make do with the famous two-seater outhouse which had been papered on the inside with marvelous covers from *The New Yorker*. We knew all the covers by heart, but visitors would become enchanted and stay inside too long. One visiting lady became—one supposes—so fascinated by the art work that she overstayed her welcome, and one of the boys, in need of the facilities, let fly with a stream against the side of the privy. The door flew open and Mrs. C. tore out with the speed of Mercury, not looking to right or to left.

For bathing the boys went into the woods where there was a forest pool fed by a mountain stream. I couldn't stand it. I just used lots of deodorant. But as soon as I landed my job as dance critic of the *Boston Herald* in 1936, I pulled my new rank and suggested that I be permitted to shower in the master's own warm-water haven. However, I stuck by *The New Yorker* outhouse until it was replaced with more modern conveniences.

Most of the boys built their own cabins in the woods. Wilbur Mc-Cormack had been one of the first. It was a simple boxlike building. When Foster joined the company, he shared it with Mac, and when

I visited I always stayed with them. Frank Overlees, of Delaware Indian descent, built a marvelous hexagonal log cabin with a wonderful stone fireplace. Frank lived in it right through the era of the men's group and even afterward when he stayed on to work for the new Festival arrangements. Denny Landers built a log cabin in another spot far from everyone else and was proud that his fireplace drew successfully. After he left, Jess Meeker moved in. Fred Hearn also had a cabin—not log—which was very grand with a privy all its own. All these buildings were on Shawn's extensive acreage, but as I've said, he never visited any one of the cabins without being invited.

Fern Helscher did not have her own cabin at first. Sometimes she stayed at the farm with Shawn, but more often she roomed at Greenwater Lodge, on Greenwater Pond (actually, a sizable lake), owned by the Sam Houstons. Mrs. Houston always had a big pot of coffee in the back of the old coal stove, and I remember that whenever anyone was hungry, there always seemed to be blueberry muffins or breakfast cake or something good available to all who entered that cheery kitchen.

Fern was essential to the Pillow, to the men's group, to Ted Shawn. Her summer salary at first was one dollar spending money per week. She cooked some meals over the fireplace. She picked blueberries and sold them on the streets of nearby Lee. She got sick and tired of eating baked beans. But she believed in Ted Shawn and in his Men Dancers. Her official job was press agent—and occasionally booker—and she was one of the best in the business. Indeed, she and Isadora Bennett for many years were the top dance press agents in America.

Fern was not a beautiful woman, but she was an attractive one. Her figure was handsome, and her bosom and legs spectacularly gorgeous. One summer, when a road gang was providing tar topping for the old Pillow road, Shawn mentioned to her that the paving was stopping about one hundred feet short of the Pillow driveway and that his pleas to town officials to extend the service farther had fallen on deaf ears. So many feet had been budgeted and that was that. Fern said, "Let me handle this." She put on a white sharkskin pants suit (long before ladies wore same), with a daring top that was slashed almost to the navel. She topped it with a Chinese coolie hat tilted at a rakish angle. She fixed a huge pitcher of icy martinis, trotted down the road to where the workmen were just about to complete their assigned job, and stopping at the line to which Shawn wanted the road extended, she called, "Boys! If you build the road to this line, you can have everything you see just beyond it." They bent to the task like madmen, reached the line, and as they did, Fern deposited the martinis in the road and ran like hell to the farmhouse.

Fern's background as a reporter and as one long associated with the wire services was of enormous help in promoting Ted Shawn and his Men Dancers. She was gregarious, friendly, and witty. She told me about the time she went into the office of one of the major Midwest newspapers to promote a Shawn appearance. The city editor and some of his staff knew Fern and took her out to lunch. They asked, "What the hell are you representing a bunch of fairies for?" "They're not fairies, but let's not talk about them. They're my job and I like 'em, so what have you been up to?" They gossiped for an hour, then Fern got up to leave. "Here's a batch of pictures of 'the fairies.' If you can do anything about it, fine. If not, okay. Thanks. See ya." The next day, a full Shawn spread on page one; the first time an artist had ever hit that front page since Paderewski had played there years before.

Booking was a sideline, but she was good at it. Toward the end of the Men Dancers era, she dropped by a university office where student entertainment series were planned. "Got your dance attraction yet?" she asked. The administrator said yes, they were committed to the new team of Miriam Winslow (a former pupil of Shawn's who had helped run Boston Denishawn) and Foster Fitz-Simons (Foster had left the Shawn group the season before to become Winslow's partner). Did Fern know them? Yes. "And how lucky you are to have them. They're marvelous. When have you booked them here? Isn't that odd. You know Ted Shawn was their teacher. He's very proud of them. And he happens to have an open date at just that time. You haven't actually signed the contract? Well, why take the students when you can have the master?" Fern got the booking. Isadora Bennett, who handled Winslow and Fitz-Simons, cursed Fern heartily. "But it was fair," she said, "like love and war. Fern had the product."

Fern also did advance for the troupe's London engagement at His Majesty's Theatre. British critics, always ballet-oriented—they had taken years to accept Duncan and St. Denis—had their reservations about the all-male experiment, but they treated the project seriously. Arnold Haskell, the distinguished ballet critic and author, found "self-imposed limitations" in the concept of the all-men programs except in the tribal dances—"These are truly brilliant because they are creative, building up a theatrical atmosphere and not just stating an ethnographic truth." He felt that "the Shawn method [was] to be seen at its best in *Labour Symphony*" and at its worst in *The Hound of Heaven* (based on the Francis Thompson religious poem and with a score by Meeker): "This quasi-dramatic representation of soul-state was almost too much for the gravity of an English audience which cannot take mere 'uplift' seriously." But for the rest, Haskell concluded, "Better ensemble training I have seldom seen."

At home *Labor Symphony*, created for the second tour of the men's group, was a great favorite. It dealt with the actions of men in the fields, on the sea, in the forests, and in the factories. Some critics hailed it as a perfect example of Shawn's "genius as a choreographer" and found it to be both "beautiful" and "masculine." *The Hound of Heaven*, on the other hand, was never popular. Shawn would not admit that it was a flop. It was endless in length, and he flew about the stage in a cape, which he discarded to reveal himself with not much on. He wore a poetic black wig, and he posed, crouched, and climbed about a sort of altar. He always said that mail proved it to be important to those with sensitivity and that it had actually affected the lives of some viewers. The late Charles Weidman, who did devastating takeoffs of dancers—Martha, Doris, himself, Tamiris, Miss Ruth (doing her *Cobras* with an enema tube and wearing eyeglasses), a Duncan dancer, etc.—included Shawn's *Hound* by wearing white flannel underwear and a bright green jockstrap and sucking in his stomach violently every time he swung the cape away to reveal his body.

I told Shawn about Charles's satires and suggested he should see them. He knew that Charles was a great mimic and agreed that takeoffs of Miss Ruth and Martha would be hilarious. When I told him that Charles had one about him, he looked surprised and said, "I can't imagine what he would do. I don't do anything that anyone could possibly satirize." I took him to see it. He pretended to laugh, but he didn't think it was very funny.

He and the boys worked hard, not only at dance, at Jacob's Pillow. They planted gardens, they painted buildings, they built roads, they dug cesspools. The boss worked about as hard as anyone, although he did choose what jobs he'd do. But anyone who ever received a letter from him had read on endless occasions how many hours he "mixed and poured cement" or "laid flagstones" and the like.

He also, for those days, paid his dancers well. When the moderns were settling for ten dollars a performance—later, it was slightly more—Shawn was paying his dancers more than union scale. He loathed unions and when he was approached about unionizing his troupe, he asked what union minimum was. When told, he snapped, "I pay more." His guarantee of year-round maintenance for all the boys was of course also unheard of.

When the cycle of the Men Dancers came to a close on May 7, 1940, at Symphony Hall in Boston, Ted Shawn felt that he had accomplished his mission of proving that men could and should dance. The Selective Service Act had been passed, and he knew that most of the men would be in the armed forces before long. Partly, although he would never admit it, he was running out of ideas for all-male programs.

The final tour carried three complete programs. One of them was characterized by a potpourri of dances from earlier years plus dances choreographed by some of the boys themselves—permission for this would never have been granted by Shawn a few seasons earlier. There were dances choreographed by the company's first soloist, Barton Mumaw, and by Fred Hearn, the Delmar twins (Frank and John), Sam Steen, and even by the composer-pianist Jess Meeker. The concluding *Jacob's Pillow Concerto* was a joint choreographic effort of everyone. There had, of course, been summer workshop pieces choreographed by the boys. Foster, with the strongest choreographic leanings, had worked at the Pillow, and Dennis, among others, had tried his hand at choreography. But Shawn remained the master choreographer, the master teacher and, indeed, the master of the company and of Jacob's Pillow.

When it was all over, the dancers who had been long in Shawn's service were given either a substantial (for those days) cash reward (or severance pay) or a parcel of Jacob's Pillow land. Frank took the land, and for several summers, until he married and moved into Stockbridge, I would stay in his, the handsomest and most elaborate of the cabins. Barton, Jess, Fred, Frank, John Schubert and most of the others did military duty. Mac made the army his career; Johnny was killed (missing in action).

The last tour, 1939 to 1940, was a memorable one. There was an unprecedented (for dance) one-week stand in Philadelphia with rave reviews capped by "Magnificent achievement technically and choreographically—faultless dancing." The New York farewell at Carnegie Hall was impressive. Louis Biancolli in the *World-Telegram* went into ecstasies over Shawn's choreographic treatment of the Bach *Toccata and Fugue in D Minor*, and in the *Herald Tribune* I wrote that "one could wish it had been a debut instead of a good-bye." The very last performances in Boston had the traditionally reserved Bostonians standing, stomping, clapping, and cheering.

The statement to the press which Shawn prepared on the occasion of the disbanding of the company was typical of the belligerent ego which made him push beyond the bounds of either good taste or good sense. It began, "Shawn, always the pioneer, feels that he has achieved magnificently what he set out to do with the men's group. . . . Now Shawn is eager to get at still newer and bigger things. . . ." The in-between blurbs are just as rich in self-praise and self-appraisal.

There were still more dancing years left to Ted Shawn, but as he entered his fifties, he began thinking about extending his own dancing self into a younger body. He had always been a superb teacher, but no matter whom he taught, he reserved for himself the post of star. Now he was willing to groom someone else not just for stardom but as his replacement. That someone was Barton Mumaw.

Barton had danced with Denishawn at the Lewisohn Stadium, headed the ensemble of the Men Dancers, and had earned a big following for himself on the tours of the Shawn Men Dancers in solos created especially for him by Shawn. He was quite unlike his mentor in build, for he was very slender, lithe, darkly exotic. Ted did not try to turn him into a junior Shawn as a dancer, whatever dreams he may have had for him as head of a company, school, or institution. He created dances that celebrated Mumaw's swiftness and agility, his technical skill. He explored for him in dance both the humor and the sadness that lay within him, as well as exploiting his muscular exuberance.

The solos included the prancing, aerial-oriented, flippant *The French Sailor;* near nude, gleaming, soaring, stabbing warrior in *The Dyak Spear Dance;* the clever, somewhat supercilious creature of *Pleasantly Satiric Comment;* and, perhaps most effective of all, the hauntingly lovely, ineffably sad, *Pierrot in the Dead City.* And Barton was truly a knockout as a dancer. It was logical, then, that when the cycle of the Shawn Men Dancers ended and Barton had completed his military duties in the United States Army in World War II, Shawn should try to launch him on an independent career. There was talk of teaming him with Miriam Winslow, since Foster Fitz-Simons had left Winslow and returned to the University of North Carolina to live with his wife and family and pursue a teaching career. Barton danced briefly with Lisa Parnova, and this association led him to study ballet and work at it more than he had done before. But it was chiefly as a soloist that he made a bid for a major place on the dance scene.

It never really worked. Barton, as I say, was an exciting dancer, but I thought then and I feel today that he was not a strong enough, vivid enough personality to carry a solo recital. Shawn himself, as a soloist, had impact. He could carry a one-man concert not only because of a varied program—an American Indian dance, a whirling dervish, a sexy Spaniard, a clean American doing country dances, an aerial dancer (*Frohsinn*), an archaic sophisticate (*Gnosienne*), a god (*Shiva*), a savior of mankind (*Prometheus*)—but because of that presence, that electrifying "hereness" with which a stage star is endowed. I don't think Barton was, to use a vaudeville term for a comic and a straightman, a "second banana," but he was a supporting star.

This was a difficult time for me because Ted hoped that I would give Barton rave reviews in the *Herald Tribune.* I could not. There were good notices and much praise. But Ted would glower at me and say, "But you qualify everything you say about Barton." I did.

There was a second reason for this in addition to Barton Mumaw's inability to command an entire evening by himself, and that was his own choreography. Shawn had always created for and on Barton—he never superimposed himself. When Barton turned to choreography, he tended to try to don the Shawn mantle. It was too big for him. He was not the heroic type. So in some of the new dances—not in all of them—one felt the presence of a Shawn shadow, not a real Mumaw.

And something else was happening on the dance scene. The days of the solo dance recital, popular in the 1920s and into the 1930s, was over. Shawn's approach to dance—and Barton's along with it—was dated. A new dance era had arrived. The moderns were far less stark and much more theatrical than they had been, and the ballet was taking on much of the movement and dramatic expressivity of modern dance. Companies were getting bigger, productions more elaborate, dances longer. Barton, both before the war and after the war, tried hard to be the dance successor of Ted Shawn. I don't mean that he wanted to imitate him, although I myself think he did unintentionally rather like a son following in his father's footsteps or, in this case, dancesteps.

And there was the aura of the heir about Barton. He was close to Ted as protégé, companion, and appointed successor. Shawn used to delight in telling the story of a woman who launched a rumor that Barton was the illegitimate son of Ted Shawn and a Javanese princess. Indeed, with his black hair, slightly slant eyes, and somewhat masklike face, Barton didn't seem much like an ordinary American boy from Hazelton, Pennsylvania.

Barton, under Shawn's demanding aegis, tried to forge his own career, but the dominance didn't work. He broke with Shawn. At first with bitterness on the Shawn side—"disloyal" he was deemed—and tried dancing in Broadway shows, with a crack at the Indian dance in *Annie Get Your Gun* (choreographed by Tamiris, with her husband, Daniel Nagrin, as the first to dance the solo Indian role) as his most successful assignment. Eventually he turned to business for a career, although he has continued to teach dancing and perform occasionally.

But in the 1930s, Shawn had found and groomed a genuine new talent, and as long as that talent was used to enhance the period of the Men Dancers, it was enormously successful. Perhaps I can describe best what went wrong or, rather, didn't work by recalling an exchange between Ted Shawn and me. After reading one of my "qualified" reviews of Barton, Shawn said, "Why don't you say that he is the greatest dancer of the day, why don't you write that . . . etc." It went on and on. When he was finished, I looked at him and said, "Would you want me to use those words on Barton that I have always reserved for you?" I'd hit him in his ego and he backed down, but there was truth in what I said.

12

Throughout his long career Ted Shawn expended a great deal of energy protesting his own importance. Miss Ruth had said, "He should be proud of being Ted Shawn and not envious of *not* being Ruth St. Denis." All of us, at one time or another, were bored, irritated, or angry at his ceaseless promotion of himself. At the dining room table at Jacob's Pillow—first with the Men Dancers and later with the Dance Festival faculty and guests—he would hold forth on the subject of Ted Shawn. When I was there, I would try to steer him into anecdotes, for there were many of them and most were funny, and he never minded as long as he talked about himself. Once when he was driving everyone up the wall with a dissertation about himself—no one was permitted to interrupt—I looked across the table at La Meri, and I, in a very slangy adaptation of the gesture language of the Hindu dance *mudras,* said mutely, "Would you like to come with me for a drink? An eye opener?" Since I had learned *mudras* in her classes, she knew what gestures I had mastered, she got my impudent suggestion, her eyes sparkled, and with a minimized gesture, she gave an "amen to that!" So we both rose from the table and left.

In the fall of 1975 William Milié, who had been at the Pillow for five years in the remote past and who had become chief choreographer for German television in Munich as well as a choreographer for Austria's Salzburg Festival, was reminiscing with me during a quick trip to New York. Bill, in 1955, had danced the Fool—and brilliantly—in Myra Kinch's *Sundered Majesty,* a modern dance work created especially for Shawn in the role of Shakespeare's *King Lear.* Bill, looking back, remembered both the good and the bad. "I remember in *Lear* I'd start out lying unseen on the floor while Shawn,

above me, did the mad scene. I was always so impressed with the
power of Shawn's performance, physically and dramatically, that he
seemed to tune me to top dance-pitch for my own solo. I think he
identified with Lear, a king betrayed. Because he was a king himself
and he was always talking about those who were disloyal to him. I
always felt that he did not need to argue all the time and so desperately about his own greatness. His accomplishments said it all. He
didn't need to go around bad-mouthing Martha Graham. Let her say
what she wanted but he should have been above it."

Milié said, "Shawn had a great impact personally and theatrically
on me. He had a truly powerful presence. He was for many of us a
father figure, kind and generous but he sure could pull an 'I am Ted
Shawn' act when anyone crossed him."

Tony Charmoli, the Emmy Award-winning choreographer for
television, choreographer and director for the huge clubs in Las
Vegas, and stager of dance numbers for many of the most famous
singing and dancing stars, came to Jacob's Pillow in 1940 at eighteen.
He was poor, he was from a town near Minneapolis, and Ted
Shawn was the first star he had ever met. "I was totally enraptured
with him," recalled Tony in 1975. "But I don't think he influenced
my life one way or another. It was simply exposure to dance that he
and the Pillow provided." Tony was able to participate in the last
performances involving the Men Dancers at the Pillow, following the
Boston farewell as the disbanding was being implemented. "Dancing
with the few of the Men Dancers who were left gave me great experience at performance. As for Shawn, I have to be totally grateful to
him for this exposure and also for the work, the exhausting work he
offered us—yes, offered—because you never get anywhere without
work."

Mary Washington Ball was running the school at Jacob's Pillow at
the time, but Shawn was present to teach. In the choreographic
workshop Tony created two dances, one with music suggested by
Miss Ball. "The chance to do these dances, and to live dance,
breathe dance, eat dance inspired me to go on for a career. But I
don't believe Shawn influenced me choreographically. I had always
made dances. As a child I had made up my tap dances, and I was
doing it again, in my way, at the Pillow, and I simply went on fol-

lowing my own bent. I learned a lot from Shawn but I never copied him."

And Tony never did. As he admits cheerfully, in 1940 he was "absolutely numb in his presence." But I remember having cocktails with them some ten years later when Tony was already a big success as the choreographer of one of the most popular TV shows, *Your Hit Parade*. I remember that Tony, a voracious talker like Shawn, was briefly silenced when Shawn shouted, "Tony, shut up! I have something to say." In 1975 I asked Tony what had happened between his numbness and his new superarticulation. "I think you call it growing up," he said. "I grew up and knew what he was all about." I asked Tony what Ted Shawn, to him, was all about. "There was lots of dance in him, but it was always as he saw dance. I found it rather limiting. I was interested in going into what is commonly, and erroneously, called 'commercial dance.' Shawn was flashy. He was as close to commercial as he could get and still remain in the concert field. But I wanted a bigger audience and frankly I wanted more money. I'd been in the concert field after the Pillow, and I knew what it was all about. No money, and people who were concert dance then and still are today are still poor. I turned down an invitation from Martha Graham to dance in her company—I had been in her classes. I still admired Shawn then, but I found a great superiority in Martha. But I think the greatest training I had was from Hanya Holm in modern and Helene Platova in ballet. But I still wanted a bigger audience, so I declined Martha's offer."

Tony, like countless students once connected with Ted Shawn, kept in touch with him over the years. They met only sporadically, and he and Tony would embrace, reminisce, and argue. Tony had always been a maverick. He had brought his tap shoes to the Pillow. "I hadn't practiced in a long time," he said. "I was told that Mr. Shawn disapproved of tap in his educational institution. But I thought even if I did desecrate his temple, screw him, I was going to practice. I did and nothing was said. So over the years, through occasional meetings, his long, mimeographed newsletters, and his personal letters to me, we remained good friends. I probably learned more from Martha and Hanya and Platova and from Peter Hamilton, who taught me Humphrey-Weidman technique, but Shawn and the school itself provided the initial thrust to get me going and I have never forgotten that." Tony became a major force in the dance world of entertainment, and with his home and gardens in Hollywood, his Lincoln Continental, and his sports cars, he says, "And Shawn started all this for me. He was the impetus."

La Meri, a star herself and head of the Pillow's ethnic dance department, found collaboration with Shawn rewarding and infuriating. In 1975 still busy directing, choreographing, and teaching at seventy-seven, she said, "It was twenty good years of roaring, bloody battles." She, at his insistence, choreographed for him, adapting East Indian and Spanish techniques to his style in occasional productions such as *El Amor Brujo,* and he put her in a retrospective ballet evocative of Denishawn, a bad piece which he said he had done especially for me because I had never seen a Denishawn performance for Denishawn had ended before I ever saw concert dancing. He was hurt that I didn't like it. (Miss Ruth said it was not true Denishawn—"It was just the trappings, not the art," she snorted.)

I have seen La Meri pacing the entire parking lot at Jacob's Pillow, her tail twitching like that of an enraged cat. I'd stop the car, lean out, and yell, "What's the matter?" The answer, "That man! I could kill him!"

Once, at the faculty dining table he announced, toward the end of a festival season, that he would like to have a faculty meeting where members could make suggestions about improving Jacob's Pillow. Both La Meri and Myra Kinch, with her composer-pianist husband, Manuel Galea, had ideas but were afraid to make any suggestions. Antony Tudor, on the faculty that year, urged them to do so. Tudor, who always enjoys stirring up mini- or maxidramas, said with a sly, sardonic smile that he was sure that Ted was serious about wanting really honest suggestions. Laughing satanically, "I'm convinced," he convinced them. So at the meeting they made their suggestions about college credits, revised curriculum, and doing away with teacher training, which were greeted stonily. Myra was not invited to return to the Pillow the following year, although she had become almost a permanent fixture there, because she had been in Shawn's words "disloyal" and "inharmonious." He needed La Meri, but he shortened her teaching period, and it was at that time he said to me that he could forgive her (but not Myra) because she was obviously in the throes of menopause and "not responsible."

Later, when I talked to them, I said, "Are you out of your minds? Tudor was egging you on just for the fun of the explosion. You know Ted didn't want any suggestions. You've known him long enough for that." Myra said, "Well, why did he ask for them?" And I answered, "You were supposed to suggest pink toilet paper for the girls' cabins because it would be more feminine, and La Meri was supposed to suggest that her classes in *mudras* be held in the smaller studio instead of the bigger one because the atmosphere would be more like a temple. And he would have agreed and told everyone that Jacob's Pillow was cooperative and that your valuable suggestions were a part of the constantly improving program at Jacob's Pillow." They agreed with me. Myra, shown the error of her ways, returned after her "sabbatical" because Ted Shawn needed her.

Ted Shawn's relationship to my own career became less influential with the passing years. But I shall never forget his initial encouragement or his help. When I graduated from the University of North Carolina in 1935 with a major in drama, a minor in music, and a total involvement with dance (and not one college credit to show for that), I couldn't get a job. The family—mother, father, sister—was in New Canaan, but a very devoted aunt, who had sent me seven fifty a week for food (and I made it do) while I was in college, gave me something like ten dollars a week to stay in New York and try my hand at writing. I spent four dollars a week for a room, the rest went for food, and I somehow managed to cadge free dance lessons. I wrote and wrote about dancing but with no buyers. I learned a lot about writing from a long-time friend of my aunt and my mother. She was Dorothy Reid, a successful writer of magazine articles. I learned more about "expository writing" (as it was called to distinguish it from "creative") from her than I ever did in college. I sold my first article—it was a plea for dance training for boys in college, and I called it "Football Heroes Groan"—to *The Dance Magazine* (run in those days by Robert Milton and Anatole Chujoy), and I know they took it because Dot Reid had made me write and rewrite that piece until I was in tears.

Shawn, during the same very lean period, had written a series of twenty-seven articles on the history and various aspects of dance for the *Boston Herald*. I didn't know then that the owner of the *Herald* was Sidney Winslow, Jr., Miriam Winslow's father, and that Ted had probably gotten the assignment because Mimi knew Ted was short of money and because of her Denishawn association with him. She was always helpful and generous with him, giving him teaching jobs at her school during the lean Springfield College days, engaging him for a concert or two, making donations to Jacob's Pillow, but he was never grateful. He never really forgave her for taking Foster away from him to be her partner, although he must certainly have known that Foster was ready to find a place for himself as a principal dancer and choreographer. Certainly she was instrumental in getting Shawn the *Herald* assignment.

The writing job was not simply a dole. Ted Shawn was a professional writer. His books included his first effort, *Ruth St. Denis: Pioneer and Prophet; The American Ballet*, a series of provocative essays on his view of dance history, his restatements of various forms of dance, and his vision of an American "ballet" which would not have Russian or European or even classical technique foundations; and *Gods Who Dance*, a book about the dances he had seen and learned during the Oriental tour. Furthermore Shawn had a large and devoted Boston following. So the *Herald* was getting something for its money. It got more than it had anticipated, for the series sold out completely. This convinced the tough but aristocratic managing editor, Robert Choate, that perhaps there was a reading public for dance. Shawn wrote me about the success of his series and suggested that "the time to strike is now."

I went to Boston and struck. Mr. Choate was not interested—I had had no experience. How did he think I'd get experience if no one gave me a start? Well, I went to his office again and again, each time with a different idea for dance coverage. Suddenly, during one visit, he said, "For God's sake, go to Bennington but get out of here. I'll pay you." The pay was thirty-five dollars for three stories. I turned in about one story a week and my pay averaged $11.67 per week. I lived on it. I was quite slim.

My first article came from Bennington, where I reviewed the debut of Lincoln Kirstein's Ballet Caravan, a sort of younger relation of George Balanchine's and Kirstein's American Ballet, their first company. My second piece was about Ted Shawn and his Men

Dancers at Jacob's Pillow, and from there on I reviewed the moderns at Bennington and the Shawn activities.

Shawn's first attempt to muzzle me or control my writing came with the interview I did with Martha Graham at Bennington. It was an interview, not a review, and I simply reported what she said about dance. Shawn was furious and accused me of being in "the enemy camp." I pointed out that it was an interview and it was my job to report what Martha had said, not what I felt. He looked at me and snapped, "But you're tacitly upholding a horrible lie." The "lie" was simply that she had stated her own theories. Foster and I howled delightedly over that remark and "tacitly upholding" something horrible became a sort of gag with us.

In 1938 I received a letter that was designed to put me in my place. I had written something which had displeased him and I received the following: I should "not set [myself] up as God Almighty to instruct creative artists who by their very nature are of a higher order of being to any critic that ever lived." In a letter a few weeks later he was a bit kinder in his distinction between the master race and the servants: "I know I am expecting something of you that should not be expected this early. You are growing and that is fine, but you are also passing through in your critical career the stages analagous to the measles and mumps in childhood."

He never failed, of course, to tell me what he expected of me in specific areas. That same year he chided, "In your review of Kirstein's book, *Blast at Ballet*, you fail to mention his inexcusable omission of any discussion of me, and of the similar failure in his earlier big book, although verbally you told me you felt he was wrong, and here was an admirable opportunity to right this wrong." Actually I had talked to Lincoln, who was very enthusiastic about my reviews when I was first starting, about the omission of Shawn and St. Denis in the first edition of his superb book, *The Dance* (later issued as *The Book of the Dance*). His explanation was that since Shawn was such an expert writer himself and had written and published so much on Denishawn, there was no need for him to add anything. But I pointed out that his book was a history and whether he approved of Denishawn or not it was still a major element in American dance development. "Besides," I said, "Noverre was also a writer, and in his *Lettres* he described his principles better than you could do, so why

the hell did you include a long section on him in your book?"
"Right," said Lincoln, and in the next edition of *The Dance* there was
a big new section on the Denishawners.

In 1962 after reading reviews by John Martin and myself on the
newly defected and dazzling Rudolf Nureyev, Shawn wrote, "I
thought your article was much, much nearer the truth (that always
means it came the nearest to being *my* opinion!)." So he did have his
disarming moments of humorous insight into himself.

In the midst of one of his long letters to me there was one sharp
paragraph. It was about Doubleday's publication of the *1001 Night
Stands* book that Gray Poole had edited and rewritten for him and
which Doubleday was publishing: "I read what you wrote about
1001 Night Stands with acrid interest. I realize you are one of those
charming, seemingly gentle people who have a quiet determined way
of doing just what they please! It's in God's hands—only He can
deal with Walter Terry, and even He has a job at that!"

This exchange between dancer and critic on a personal level went
on from 1936 right to the end. Sometimes there would be very de-
tached, coolly intellectual outlines on the function of a critic. Often
there were "bravos!" for what I had written and there were also
blasts. He was occasionally given to saying that an adverse criticism
had been helpful. He was furious at my initial review of that solo
called *The Whirlwind*, and we argued about it over lunch. He went
into elaborate detail about how it was constructed, what he did in it,
and why it was perfect. When he had finished, I said, "You've convinced me." He sighed. "You've convinced me," I added, "that at-
mospherically it is a perfect whirlwind. But it's still a lousy dance."
Later he agreed I was right and that the criticism was helpful. He
dropped it and replaced it midway on tour with a new number,
Dance of the Liberated Soul. I didn't like it either, and I must confess I
skirted reviewing it. He was very hurt and wrote that he had done
what I had suggested and now I'd ignored his efforts.

But when he did take advice, which wasn't often, he'd often do
the wrong thing. Toward the end of the Men Dancers days, his age
was beginning to show. His hair had been thinning and graying
when I had first met him. Now, despite attempts at dieting, he was
heavy, and he was no longer as agile as he had been. Still, he used a
very youthful, "pretty" makeup and blackened his hair (including a

painted hairline) to jet. He wouldn't listen to subtle suggestions. Behind his back, everyone was distressed, including his dancers, about what he looked like on stage. He wore the same brief trunks as his boys, but his rear was heavier, and there was a roll, even when he sucked in the stomach, about the middle. I finally said to him, "You know you're asking for it with that makeup and compared with the boys. People are saying you looked twenty-six from the neck up and forty-six from the neck down. Why don't you look like a glorious forty-six which would make every middle-aged man envious?" His feelings were hurt. I received a letter from him saying he knew that comparison with the boys was made and that he danced with them only to strengthen his battle for men in dance. But that he would do something about the black hair. He did. The makeup remained pure movie star, but on his head he wore a shiny, silver, marcelled wig, or else he whitened his own hair so that it gleamed like sequins on a white dress. It was awful! But he had tried.

He was always "filling me in" on "the truth." He felt that neither John Martin nor Miss Ruth gave him credit for what were his accomplishments before, during, and after Denishawn. He understood that I was forced to rub elbows with "anti-Shawnites," but he felt that if I knew "the truth," I would see that justice was done. This was a constant theme.

He was disappointed when I could not take his manuscript autobiography and remake it into *1001 Night Stands*. I tried with two sample chapters of anecdotes, but he was not happy with the result and said with full justification that what I had come up with was more St. Denis than Shawn. But it was supposed to be a book of anecdotes, and Miss Ruth could be very, very funny. She had a fabulous sense of humor. Ted Shawn did not. He had a sense of fun, but not of humor. So I pleaded that for the sake of my career, I must do a book that was wholly mine and not just a supporting job of work for him. This let us both off the hook, and Gray Poole did the job.

But as the years went by, there was no question but that I would be his official biographer. In his letters he would say that I must spend hours with him going over the clippings and notices and pictures. He'd outline Denishawn events year by year. He'd write, "There is still that big box I want you to go through," or, "If you want another session with me, taping or not taping, please give me your free dates," and toward the end, "Glad about your news of finishing the book *Miss Ruth* so soon. Glad you will let me read the galleys of parts of it that involve me; glad of the idea of your doing my biography next (gives real point to the taping sessions)." And in a piece I wrote called "The Anniversaries of Ted Shawn" in which I tried to separate his accomplishments by himself from his accomplishments in collaboration with others, he wrote to say that his favorite phrase in the piece was "on his own." The last time I talked to him by phone, he was in his beloved winter home in Eustis (he had told me the summer before that he never wanted to go back to Jacob's Pillow again), and the biography came up. He said, while coughing constantly with that emphysema which hastened his end, "If you want to pump the old man for anything more for the book, you'd better hurry. There isn't much time. . . ."

He was concerned not only about securing his stature in history but also about the continuation of his projects after he had gone. With the end of the era of Ted Shawn and his Men Dancers his incredible energies, determination, and imagination went into the building of the Jacob's Pillow Dance Festival and School. He came to think of this as a physical legacy, as something he had begun which could continue.

He almost lost control of the Pillow at one point while he was away on a tour, but La Meri, a member of the board of directors, was able to save the situation by her vote, for there was a moment when it seemed as if Shawn would not be reengaged as the Pillow's director. He saw to it at once that such a situation would never again arise by instituting membership changes assuring, as the years went on, a docile board.

As his own performing activities decreased, especially with respect to touring—he did an enormously successful Australian solo tour in 1947 (fifty solo recitals in five cities) and made a United States tour with his Jacob's Pillow Dance Company in 1952—the festival become more and more important to him. He danced frequently, of course, for his festival—his old solos (*Thunderbird, Japanese Spear*, and, to the very last, his *A Study of St. Francis*) and three Myra Kinch dances tailored to his increasing physical limitations—and he choreographed for the students at the Pillow (*Minuet for Drums* and *Mountain Whippoorwill*, among others).

His dance prejudices quickly faded as his own performing and choreographic activities took second place to his duties as a director of what was to become the summertime center for dance in America and the world's most illustrious dance festival. He knew that we had come into a ballet age, so he began to make ballet artists the key attraction on almost every program. The programs themselves, initially given only on Fridays and Saturdays, were extended in time to nearly a week, Tuesdays through Saturdays, and with a season lasting ten weeks.

The "teas" had been held in the barn studio which, by the time Ballet Theatre played there, had been doubled in size. It was still on one level (except for a tiny elevated viewing booth seating about twelve people) in the back, with half the floor space for the audience and the other half for the performers who had to make their exits and entrances either from the tea garden or the wild woods beyond. It was intimate but its rustic facilities did not discourage stars. I remember a stellar performance by Ruth St. Denis, Ted Shawn, Markova and Dolin, America's and England's most celebrated dance duos. While Markova was dancing her gentle *To a Water Lily* to the equally gentle music of MacDowell, Miss Ruth was changing out of sight but within hearing into an East Indian nautch costume, ankle bells and all. The bells jangled throughout Markova's dance, and as she floated offstage and into the woods with her exquisite *pas de bourrées*, I heard her mutter, "This number should have been titled *The Lotus!*"

On July 9, 1942, the Ted Shawn Dance Theater, designed by Joseph Frantz, the architect for the symphonic shell at Tanglewood, opened with Shawn dedicating his 500-seat theater by dancing *The Doxology* and his *Four American Folk Dances*. It was an exciting event, for this was the first theater to be designed expressly for dance. It was constructed to look like a huge New England barn, the beams were enormous, the roof was capped by a wrought iron silhouette of Barton in his *Bourrée* solo with music by Bach, and the theater was connected with the big barn studio which had served for so long as a make-do theater. The studio, incidentally, was linked in L-shape fashion with another hundred-year-old barn unit, which was used as a storeroom and as a sort of recreation room. In the days of the Men Dancers it was always called No. 9, in memory, I was told, of a Japanese whorehouse that some (or perhaps several) Denishawners had visited or heard about during the Oriental tour. No. 9, the studio, and the theater framed three sides of the old "tea" area with its lawn, its stage-size platform for sunning or rehearsing. It was on this platform in 1941 that Miss Ruth's historic *Radha*, revived thirty-five years after its première, was filmed in color by Dwight Godwin, another historic moment, for the ensemble of young priests was headed by a junior Ballet Theatre dancer, Donald Saddler, destined to become a successful, Tony Award–winning Broadway choreographer.

I remember that day well. Miss Ruth was past sixty, but she looked gorgeous in her golden headdress, a jeweled bodice, a golden nautch skirt, and a still slim bare midriff. Her legs were heavy, so when she had to dance with the skirt off, she either moved very quickly, stood in profile or, frontward, held a position known in vaudeville as "Greek knees," that is, with the feet slightly apart and one knee turned in toward the other, giving a slimming effect.

On the second day of shooting Miss Ruth was on her dais in the blazing sun and Ted walked by, looking neither right nor left and ignoring her completely. She glanced up as the figure passed by and, before the shooting started, beckoned to me. She whispered, "I forgot I was supposed to have dinner with him last night, and I just went off to the movies. Send him to me, dear." I tracked him down sulking nearby and said, "Your wife would like a word with you." He walked back, face frozen, and stood in front of her. "Yes?" She reached for his hand. "Teddy, as you know I have always been forgetful. Usually what I forget is very trivial, but once in a while in my life I forget important things and, darling, you just happened to be one of them."

With the theater complete the debuts and the premières became of national and sometimes international importance. Shawn himself introduced the Royal Danish Ballet to America by importing Twelve leading Dancers of the Royal Danish Ballet to dance at the Pillow. Because of the tremendous success of this unit Columbia Artists Management subsequently brought over the entire Royal Danish Ballet to America to be succeeded in later years by S. Hurok as manager.

Besides being made a Knight of Danneborg by King Frederik IX of Denmark in 1957, Shawn was also accorded the signal honor of being invested by the king himself at the royal palace in Copenhagen. The Danish monarch, although he received any of his subjects in audience, never received a foreigner other than a head of state or an ambassador in official ceremonies. But Shawn was accorded the honor, perhaps because the old king, an accomplished musician, was very fond of his Royal Ballet. Shawn was coached in matters of protocol and instructed to back away from the royal presence when the king ended the audience. Shawn told me (and everyone else!) that King Frederik chatted with him about dancing for ten minutes, and as Shawn was leaving and moving backward, offered the helpful comment, "The knob of the door is on the left." Shawn, quickly realizing that the king had never backed away from anyone in his life and was simply giving directions as *he* saw the situation, reached back with his *right* hand and there was the knob! He used to say that only a dancer would have thought of that.

He also, putting up a ten thousand dollar guarantee, imported Britain's oldest ballet company, the Ballet Rambert, to America for the first time. The National Ballet of Canada made its United States debut at the Pillow, and the Royal Winnipeg Ballet made its first major United States appearances at the Pillow, as did Montreal's Les Grands Ballets Canadiens. In addition to companies, major ballet stars from abroad also graced Pillow program in *pas de deux* and *divertissements*. American ballet was by no means neglected and many junior ballet artists got their first chance at stellar assignments at Jacob's Pillow.

This shift in his attitude about ballet was based on practicality. America had entered a ballet age, and with the establishment of American or American-based ballet companies even the themes of ballets were proudly American: Agnes de Mille's *Rodeo*, Catherine Littlefield's *Barn Dance*, Eugene Loring's *Billy the Kid*, or young Jerome Robbins's *Fancy Free* being prime examples of non-Russian ballet. Mainly, ballet was box office, and as the man who wanted to make a financial go of Jacob's Pillow, Ted Shawn was willing to present ballet, American or Russian. Besides, since he himself was dancing less and less, the male ballet virtuoso was no longer a rival to him.

So, for a man who had felt ballet was foreign and for foreigners,

Ted Shawn, as impresario, changed his tune. As student enrollment increased at the school, which he labeled grandly University of the Dance, more housing was needed and the new cabins for the girls were named after ballerinas: Inge Sand (Denmark), Cia Fornarolli (Italy), Alicia Markova (England), Alexandra Danilova (Russia), Nora Kaye (America), and later Maria Tallchief, with each containing an autographed toe shoe! Miss Ruth, hearing about the new cabins and their names, purred nastily, "Interesting, dear, considering all his antiballet preachments. Ah, well, not even a St. Denis tool shed." Shawn heard about it and built a new studio, big enough for dress rehearsals and workshop programs, gave it a foyer with St. Denis posters and a gallery of St. Denis photos by her favorite photographer, Marcus Blechman, and called it Ruth St. Denis Hall.

The pattern for a given bill at the Pillow was to have one-third ballet, one-third modern, one-third ethnic dance. It wasn't a fast rule—sometimes there would be an all-ballet week or an all-Spanish dance week, or mime replacing modern—but that was the usual format. New works were encouraged, and during the period of his directorship, about thirty years, there were close to three hundred world premières, ranging from major productions to very simple, forgettable pieces. There was never a year when black dancers were not participants, and there would always be some very special and rarely seen events, such as India's great Balaraswati or the almost legendary Carmelita Maracci from California, who would rather dance for friends than for a paying public. Even Martha Graham, after declining many invitations from Shawn, gave a lecture at the Pillow, and Charles Weidman and his company were welcomed back to Papa Shawn's bosom.

And so Jacob's Pillow, built from teas in an old Yankee barn into performances of international dazzle for audiences numbering almost forty thousand per season, was the crowning achievement in the long Shawn career. But, by the mid-1960s, decline and decay set in as the entire summer circuit theater enterprise slackened everywhere, as expenses mounted, and as the Shawn grip faltered. For the decades of the thirties, forties, and fifties constituted a period when nothing whatever was happening during summertimes in New York or Boston, London or Paris in the theater and especially with dance. Dancers needed the equivalent of the actors' summer stock, and even the top stars were eager to work. The Pillow provided them with that work and at good fees plus prestige and, even more, reviews by major newspapers. As a dance critic of a major metropolitan newspaper, I had to justify a year-round salary by working the year round. Dance in New York started about Columbus Day and wound up in March. True, seasons began earlier and closed later as the summertime theater in the big cities grew. But June, July, and August were dead. I went to Jacob's Pillow every week (and to Bennington too) for the *Herald Tribune*, so I justified my salary, the star dancers kept their names before the public, and newcomers who might never have been reviewed in the *Times* or *Trib* or even in some of the other city newspapers (Boston, Albany, etc.) had a taste of the big time.

But with the mid-1960s the need, as I say, was gone, and Shawn had problems programing. He was ill and aging and not well enough to talent-scout Europe and America as he once did. He stayed closeted at the Pillow in the summer and basked in his garden in Eustis, Florida, in the winter. Of course he got around to performances when he could, but it was an effort. And during the very last years he would shake his head and wonder aloud how much longer he could go on. But he was tenacious. John Martin years before had described him as indomitable. He was that. But who would succeed him? At first it was certain that Barton, whom he had trained and guided and shared his life with for many years, would be the heir. But after World War II and with Barton's own need to carve a career for himself, the line of descent was changed, and John Christian, a nondancer but a gifted young man in matters of stage design, became Shawn's personal representative in 1949–50, the stage manager, and later the technical director of the Ted Shawn Theater and finally associate and lastly executive director of Jacob's Pillow.

In each period Ted Shawn had designated his heir to Jacob's Pillow endeavors and of course went into some detail in letters to me. In 1944 he wrote to me: "My plans for post-war life are nil—except that Barton and I have agreed to spend his first year out of the army in Eustis, getting him rested and reconditioned physically, mentally, emotionally, before either of us ever plan or attempt to do anything. Of course that year will include a summer for both of us at the Pillow, as he must assume his rightful place as associate director and begin to take over some of the burden and responsibility toward

that day when I must retire and he takes over the whole job." Barton
was stationed in England at that time and I was on duty in Egypt.

From 1949 John Christian was being groomed to take over the
burden and the responsibility of the Pillow. Briefly, in 1957, when
his brother offered him a tempting job, and again in 1959, when his
mother was urging him to take over his late father's position as head
of the family hardware store on Long Island, Chris was led into a situation that required him to consider alternatives in his own future.
The decision was not easy, but he finally decided to cast his lot with
the future of Jacob's Pillow and, with it, the heavy responsibilities
attendant on serving Ted Shawn.

As his own end drew near, Shawn wrote me, "The Pillow is not
Shawn and Shawn is not the Pillow . . . and unless you want the
Pillow to fold with my death, then I think it is up to you to get
behind Chris and help him all you can. . . ."

But somehow, with the fabulous eightieth birthday party which
Genevieve Oswald, curator of the Dance Collection of the New
York Public Library, had arranged for him, it was clear to everyone
there that he was near the end of his life, and it was equally clear to
those who thought about it, that it was the end of an era in American dance. His dancing life had spanned sixty years, from 1911 to
1971. Miss Ruth had lived to a greater age and had danced longer. It
is unarguable, I think, that of the two she was the greater artist, the
genius of the family. But although she remained active until the end
of her long life—she was a professional dancer for seventy-five
years—her influence upon the dance world ended with Denishawn;
whatever remained after was her rare personal magic as a performer
and, in truth, as a "presence" onstage and off. Ted, after Denishawn, forged a career not only for himself but, more important, for
men dancers everywhere. No one else had done it before, and it is
unlikely that anyone other than Ted Shawn, with a worldwide professional reputation as a virile male dancer, could have battled, in the
1930s, the violent American prejudice against male dancers and won.

And yet again, when the male dance experiment was terminated
with its very real triumph made evident in the swiftly increasing
numbers of boys asking for, demanding, insisting upon, and getting
undreamed of dance opportunities in schools and colleges and studios, in dance groups, large and small, and in time in television,

another quarter century of service lay ahead. When he started with the male troupe, the only major American modern dance company with men dancers was the Humphrey-Weidman company and that was because Charles was a man (trained earlier by Shawn); even Charles said that he and Doris recruited their men mainly "from relatives" because there was no place else to find them. The groups of Graham, Holm, Tamiris were all-female at that point.

The next twenty-five years after the disbanding of the male dancers saw Shawn bring a dance festival of world-wide significance into being. He built it, from small beginnings, into the biggest and the best, and I doubt that there will ever be another to equal it, partly because the need for it has diminished. But in its time it gave jobs to hundreds of dancers; it gave training to thousands of students; it interrelated, through the juxtaposition of festival and school, performing experience and education. It was one of several enterprises—the regional ballet movement evolving in the 1950s and developing into more than two hundred regional ballet companies was a related force—which helped decentralize the dance art and prove that Broadway was not the only Mecca in the dance world.

Ted Shawn's record of achievement, then, is enormous and it is unique. This in spite of the fact that he did not possess in his dancing body and but rarely in his choreography the inexplicable gift of genius that his wife, Ruth St. Denis, or his pupil Martha Graham possessed. But he was every bit as much a Titan of dance as they were. Tragically for him, he was not the Titan in those areas in which he so desperately wanted to excel. Miss Ruth had been right when she said that "he should be proud of being Ted Shawn and not envious of *not* being Ruth St. Denis," and she added, "I never could have done what he did with dancing for men. I could never have run a dance festival. And I don't believe there would ever have been a Denishawn without him . . . but still, he's jealous of me."

Bill Milié was right too when he said that Shawn did not need to protest his greatness constantly, that his accomplishments spoke for him. Tony Charmoli felt the same and so have countless others who knew him, respected him, loved him, and were almost continuously infuriated or left defeated by his behavior.

In 1936 John Martin, who never liked Ted Shawn very much, described him superbly in his book, *America Dancing:* "Keen of wit, caustic of tongue, avid of interest, terrifically temperamental, of inexhaustible energy, tenacious, aggressive, indomitable, he was obviously of the stuff to break down barriers and become the first male dancer in America to achieve a position of influence and importance."

To John's dispassionate description, I say amen, although I would have said keen of "mind" rather than "wit." In the nearly forty years I knew Ted Shawn, I encountered every one of those characteristics . . . and a few others that John didn't know about and which, I hope, I have added in these pages. Have you discovered them? that he was vulnerable as well as indomitable? that he was gentle with youth as well as aggressive with his peers? that he could speak kindly as well as caustically? I discovered too that he was selfish, vain, and petty, often arrogant and frequently tasteless, but for every negative aspect there was a positive attribute, so that many of us who knew him well soon discovered that it was impossible to like him but very possible to love him, exasperations and all. In 1934, when in the midst of some kind of personal difficulties, he wrote to a close friend of his own generation, "If you love me, be with me now." Over the decades, more than one person responded to that plea, for Ted Shawn was indeed loved, if not liked, by four generations of dancers, by American dancers who would not be benefitting so richly from the present Golden Age of Dance if it had not been for a man whose remarkable accomplishments far exceeded those talents that he craved but, ironically, did not possess.

A few years after Ruth St. Denis and Ted Shawn had parted and when anger and jealousy and conflict were only of the past, Miss Ruth, following her first visit to Jacob's Pillow, wrote of her husband: "Seeing Ted from a different vantage point, I thought as I came away from the farm that no one realized his strong individuality, his splendid intelligence, his charm and personality better than I. He was a rare, a forceful person, capable of great singleness of purpose and an artist of fine concepts, carried into execution with skill and style, while underneath he was always growing spiritually, desiring passionately to find his real selfhood."

He did not ever, I think, find that selfhood, for he was truly tormented about a possible gulf between the self he was and the self he wanted to be. But just as Miss Ruth could view him with admiration and dispassion after a period of separation, it is possible for us in the world of dance, now that he is gone, to view him with increasing admiration while dispassionately recognizing his failings. And he comes out well.

Looking at the stunning chronology of his accomplishments I am brought up astounded at his vision of "what could be." Perhaps, like Prometheus, he *was* bound, in his case by the flaws and inadequacies of a less than perfect dancer's body, less than faultless artistic taste, less than creative genius. Yet, like Prometheus, he was blessed with the monumental gift of being able to foresee what the dance could be. As the Promethean Foreseer, he was indeed a Titan, as Prometheus had been, in contributing immeasurably to the freeing of dancers from the bonds of past traditions so that they might embark upon a new and greater dance age.

INDEX

181